T0171398

The Book of Revelations

A year's worth of facebook wisdom

Mia Semuta

iUniverse, Inc.
Bloomington

The Book of Revelations
A year's worth of facebook wisdom

iUniverse books may be ordered through booksellers or by contacting:

iUniverse
1663 Liberty Drive
Bloomington, IN 47403
www.iuniverse.com
1-800-Authors (1-800-288-4677)

Because of the dynamic nature of the Internet, any web addresses or links contained in this book may have changed since publication and may no longer be valid. The views expressed in this work are solely those of the author and do not necessarily reflect the views of the publisher, and the publisher hereby disclaims any responsibility for them.

Any people depicted in stock imagery provided by Thinkstock are models, and such images are being used for illustrative purposes only.

Certain stock imagery © Thinkstock.

ISBN: 978-1-4502-9295-5 (sc)
ISBN: 978-1-4502-9296-2 (ebook)

Printed in the United States of America

iUniverse rev. date: 1/27/2011

for the Red Land High School
class of 1990

Patriots 20 years later...
20 years better!

Acknowledgements

Tom Abraham, Angel Lafferty Friend, Lacy Gonzales, Beth Lynn O'Brien and **Jennifer Martin Shuey** helped me laugh and cry my way through this project. Thank you, friends, for the fast reading and scrupulous editing!

My **facebook friends** lent me their opinions and insight and without them there would have been no reason to continue to make revelations. Thank you for your commentary and loyalty to this project.

Pastiche provided encouragement to keep feeling seventeen in my mind as well as the interior illustrations. Thank you for the gift of your talent!

Heart Stomper, Rebound, Kermit, Schroeder, Douche Bag, Ass Hat, Tall Guy, et al. - you sure did give me a lot of material; hope you aren't pissed when you read this book. Of course, if you are; whatever, you know it's true...

It's been twenty years since high school, what have you learned?

rev·e·la·tion
[rev-*uh*-**ley**-shuhn]

–noun

1. the act of revealing or disclosing; disclosure.
2. something revealed or disclosed, esp. a striking disclosure, as of something not before realized.
3. *Theology* .
> **a.** God's disclosure of Himself and His will to His creatures.
> **b.** an instance of such communication or disclosure.
> **c.** something thus communicated or disclosed.
> **d.** something that contains such disclosure, as the Bible.

4. (*initial capital letter*) Also called Revelations, The Revelation of St. John the Divine. the last book in the new testament; the Apocalypse. *Abbreviation:* Rev.

source: http://dictionary.reference.com/browse/revelation

so·cial net·work
[**soh**-shuhl] [**net**-wurk]

–noun

1. a person's family, neighbors, and friends with whom they are socially involved
2. a website where one connects with those sharing personal or professional interests, place of origin, education at a particular school, etc.

source: http://dictionary.reference.com/browse/social+network

face·book
[feys] [book]

1. the most *fabulous* time suck of the 21st century

source of the definition: Mia's head

This project happened by chance. I was standing in the bathroom, staring into the mirror and trying not to scream. It was January 1, 2010 and all around me people were waking up, crawling out of bed, nursing hangovers and making resolutions for the New Year. Not me. I was gawking at the mirror having a revelation.

As the clarity began to really set in, I decided the only socially responsible thing to do was to take it to facebook. You know facebook, it's a full-time job. As with nearly all status updates worth the nanoseconds it takes to read and LOL and hit the "like" button, I wanted to be both concise and clever. This being the first day of the twentieth year of my post-high school existence, I decided to preface my bathroom revelation "20 years Post-High School Revelation #1" and the rest is history.

20 years
Post-High School
Revelation

#1

In my mind I am still 17; in the mirror I am not. What a jagged little pill that is...

The revelation that started it all! I think we all suffer from our happy little delusions from time to time. The harshest part is that I still have the spirit and joie de vivre that I did twenty years ago but I lack the energy and the physicality. Ironically, my confidence is exponentially greater now than when I had the body to back it up. I suppose that's nature's twisted little joke. Talk about, "If I knew then what I know now..." Wow.

#2

I really hate to drive but I still love Madonna. *keep on pushing my love over the borderline*

I remember that I was sitting in the parking lot at the Credit Union trying desperately to be patient and wait for someone to take pity on me so I could turn left. The cars, they just kept coming out of nowhere! At that point, I hadn't really planned to make a daily revelation but I was sitting there, singing along to the radio, and thinking how much I really hate to drive. It's a necessary function of my day and it helps me avoid being car sick, but given the option I'd much prefer to not drive. It struck me that I did not feel that way at all in high school. Back in the day I could not wait to drive, but now? Not so much. Yet, I was still a true blue Madonna fan and so revelation #2 was born.

#3

Back then I was afraid, I was petrified. I wore a smiling mask to hide the nerves inside. I spent oh so many years just hiding from myself, but now my smile is real and I'm not afraid to feel 'cause I know that I, I will survive!

This was the day I thought, "Maybe I'll make a revelation every day..." I knew I had something fun planned for the following day and I was just feeling full of piss and vinegar, as my mother used to say, so I stayed with the music theme.

#4

If you wake your sister up early on the morning of your wedding and tell her you don't want to get married, it's best to just stay home that day. Life is too short and unpredictable to spend in an unhappy marriage.

Okay, true story here. When I was a freshman in college, (the first time), I found myself nursing quite the shattered, little, stomped-on heart. In my infinite, eighteen or nineteen year-old wisdom I thought the best way to get over Heart Stomper was to throw myself into the deep-end of a rebound relationship. I know, I KNOW, stop with the judgment already! This entire project is about growth and experience and learning from my mistakes. Anyway, I never have been one to do anything half-assed so I went full-throttle, convinced myself that not only was I over Heart Stomper but also that I was in love with Rebound. Apparently, Rebound, who would ultimately prove to be just a layup, was in love with me and thought it would be a great idea to get married. My boy William Shakespeare said it best, "Lord, what fools these mortals be." So, being but a mere mortal, I said "Yes."

The night before my wedding, I did what any sane woman would do: I picked a fight with Rebound. It was going pretty well, actually, I could see the light at the end of the tunnel and I was *not* wearing a white dress! Unfortunately, my uncle, (who is a fantastic man), patched things up and I was still in the game. Dammit. I went to bed that night knowing that something was wrong and knowing I was in the express lane to disaster but having no idea how to get out of it. The next morning, I got up bright and early and went into my sister's room. She was weighing in at fourteen years of age with all of the relationship wisdom that one can garner from the eighth grade. I woke her up- no easy task, mind you. I said, "Megan, I don't want to do this; I don't want to get married!"

She looked at me, her brown eyes wide with terror, and spoke the truest words I'd ever heard up to that point in my life, "Daddy's going to kill you! Everything's paid for."

So I got married.

Truth be told, I was waiting for Heart Stomper to burst into the church right up until the very last minute and stop the wedding. Maybe I'd seen *The Graduate* one too many times or maybe my default is just to be dramatic. At any rate, of course he did not stop the wedding but my best friend did come through with a couple of bottles of champagne in the back of the church which is what fueled me down the aisle. The after-party was fun.

I tried; I really tried to be happy with Rebound. He was nice enough, and he adored me, and I didn't have to do anything except be a housewife. Oh.My.God- I was so freakin' bored! It took me a few years and, sadly, the death of my father, to realize that I was just utterly miserable. Instead of waiting for Heart Stomper or some new mistake to rescue me, I rescued myself. I went back to college, left my husband and chose dignity instead of continuing to settle for a life I thought was inevitable. I got to keep the dog, though; it wasn't a total loss.

Now, just so you know, nineteen years ago I was not the intellectual giant you know today. I was the mental equivalent of a ninety-eight pound weakling. Today, I wouldn't wake Megan in a panic to tell her I didn't want to get married; I'd text her, "pack your bags we are outta here!!"

#5

January 4, 2010

Technology has made communication so fast that you can now confuse and inadvertently piss people off at light speed.

Revelation #5 marks the first time I doubled up in a day and also explains why my Gramma quit facebook. She had read Revelation #4 and the subsequent comments, including my tongue-in-cheek retort that I hold my uncle more responsible than my sister. Gram apparently didn't have the sarcasm font installed on her computer and man-oh-day did she let me have it. She doesn't always find me quite as amusing as others do. So, Gram was off of facebook, she seriously deactivated her page, and my revelation project was already shaping up to be a real game-changer in the family.

#6

January 6, 2010

Toilets in public restrooms now flush themselves but the water that you dribble on the sink after washing your hands does not clean itself up, people! Grab a paper towel and show a little courtesy. Maybe by the time I am having 30-year Revelations...

Still reeling from the revelation debacle that led to my Gramma scolding me in front of my 300+ friends, I wasn't entirely certain that I would soldier on with my little project. However, a trip to the ladies' room in my office building changed my mind. I came out of the stall to find that, clearly, every other woman who works on that floor must be an only child who never had to share a bathroom. Ugh…

January 7, 2010

#7

Crushes are still brutal, rejection still sucks and boys are still boys. Having learned what that tastes like back in the day doesn't make the flavor any sweeter today. However, I no longer have to wonder who will buy the beer. ☺

Yeah, this was about someone specific. He knows who he is. If he actually buys this book, giving me a little royalty, maybe I'll think about changing his name to "Former Douche Bag."

January 8, 2010

#8

Global warming my ass!!!!

Do you remember the winter of 2010? Here in Central Pennsylvania it was *brutal*! Normally, I'm like a polar bear and I'm only happy when I can see my breath. This day my breath was freezing in front of my face in the shape of the letters, "WTF"! The series of blizzards that led to several feet of snow over the next few weeks really shot a hole in the global warming theory for me.

#9

I am not going to live forever and, sadly, neither will my friends.

      This was the day I had to say goodbye to my dear friend, Richard. We had worked together on the McCain-Palin campaign and I had the good fortune to have been a guest in his home less than a month before at his annual holiday party. Richard had an unexpected stroke and passed away suddenly just after Christmas. The streets of Heaven now reverberate with a loud, booming voice that was quick to laugh and always had a kind word. You are loved and you are missed, my friend. ♥

#10

Barbie dresses like a whore.

      She does.

#11

No one else notices when I have a runner in my nylons and nobody, including me, cares! ☺

      I remember the horrible feeling I used to get if there was a runner in my nylons back in the day. It was so humiliating! I really thought it was going to be the end of me. I can even remember faking being sick so I could go home from school just so nobody would see it. Now, I sometimes leave the house knowing full-well there is a runner and I just couldn't begin to give a shit.

January 12, 2010

#12

Make time for your girls. They are the ones who hold your hair back and hand you a tissue when you need it. When you're feeling full of rage or just blue, it's your girls who will pick you up, dust you off and help you get back in the game.

Although I am certain I was pissed off at a man when I wrote this, (most likely Douche Bag), the beautiful gift of time is that I no longer remember exactly why. I remember my girls, though; my girlfriends who pull me through every heart break, hiccough, stumble and free fall. There are a few fellas that I hold in esteem equally as high, too. Thanks, friends; you know who you are. ❤

January 13, 2010

#13

Just because the radio plays the song over & over and the DJs really try to convince me that it's a good song, I can still think it sucks. *Fireflies* by Owl City is a stupid freakin' song and I change the station when it comes on!

I still hate that song and I still change the station when it comes on. I also learned that my HS buddy, Chad, hates R.E.M. as a direct result of this revelation. It's made me seriously re-think our friendship.

#14

Whomever said, "It's better to have loved and lost than never to have loved at all," was full of shit and bad manners.

I was being solemn and introspective when I wrote this revelation but I was pulled from my funk in a spectacular fashion by a couple of my friends.

John commented, "Yes, but it's better to have loved and lost than to live with a psycho. Just sayin'"

To which **Tom** responded, "I think it was probably better to have hooked up and been smacked the next day because she had too much to drink and would never think of touching you sober but hey that's just me."

How could I possibly continue to wallow in self-pity after those gems? Thanks, fellas. ☺

#15

Pat Benatar was right. Love IS a battlefield. I believe there comes a time when everything just falls in line. We live and learn from our mistakes; the deepest cuts are healed by faith. ❤

I don't remember where we were going, but while Gina and I were in the car the radio station was treating us to a little Pat Benatar mini-concert. She is seriously on the short list to write the soundtrack of my life! Pat, not Gina. Gina is on the short list of fabulous co-pilots.

#16

It can get really dark & cold out there; you need to bring your own sunshine.

Sometimes we all need a little reminder.

#17

I can now appreciate the beauty of both solitude and of good company.

I spent a lot of time in my youth afraid to be alone. I wanted to be surrounded by people at all times and usually be the center of attention. Although I still enjoy the attention, I've come to enjoy my own company and I now crave alone time. I don't do anything special but I love time to putz around, sing while I fold the laundry, talk to my cats and just *be* without having to entertain anyone else. It refreshes me. I call it "going dark." Because I go dark periodically I am able to bring along a little extra sunshine to share with others when I come out of my self-imposed exile.

#18

Hitting the snooze alarm just makes me sleepier in the end and Mondays still suck.

Do you know anyone who purposely sets their alarm for more than hour before they have to get up just so they can hit the snooze button over and over? What is wrong with those people?! I'll snooze it maybe once or twice but that's about it. No matter what, though, Mondays really suck.

#19

Of course I can have my cake and eat it, too! Why on earth would I have a cake I can't eat? Carpe diem, dammit; live in the moment and choose joy because sadness will visit all of us sooner or later and we should never, ever, deny an opportunity to smile.

I mean, seriously; who has a cake but doesn't want to eat it? Okay, fine, probably not Jillian Michaels but I think you get what I'm talking about here.

#20

I don't hate country music; some of it I actually like.

I was on the turnpike on my way to Pittsburgh, (had to go for work), and I couldn't get any other radio stations to come in clearly. I now actually have my #1 pre-set knob set to Bob. ☺

Side Note: "Bob" is otherwise known as Bob 94.9, *the* Central PA country radio station.

#21
Drunk dialing/texting/e-mailing is a vicious by-product of modern society therefore all forms of communication should be connected to a breathalyzer.

Okay, so remember Douche Bag who I was whining about? Yeah, me too. Unfortunately, I remembered him after I'd had way too much to drink and I was sad and lonely in a hotel room in Pittsburgh. It was actually the next day that I thought how much I wished my blackberry came standard with a breathalyzer.

#22
I ♥ the Primanti Brothers.

Still in Pittsburgh at this point, ate one of the famous sandwiches; L♥VE!! Still can't get on board and be a Steelers' fan, but love the P Bros!

#23
I will never watch *The Tonight Show with Jay Leno* again.

This was written in direct response to the announcement that Conan O'Brien was no longer going to be the host of *The Tonight Show.* I have fallen asleep with the TV on, but I have *never* watched Jay Leno host the show again. In my opinion, the classy thing for Jay to do would have been to say "no" when they asked him to come back. Period.

#24

I really wish I would have written down the funny one I thought of last night. Uh-oh, maybe that's the revelation...

Seriously, I thought of something hysterical and insightful but failed to write it down. If ever there was a more glaring example of aging I've never seen it.

#25

Back in the day I didn't actually memorize the anatomy of a cell- plant or animal. I cheated on the quiz. I have never been in a situation where that knowledge was necessary. I'm letting go of that guilt.

Honestly, I remember sitting in Biology class in tenth grade thinking how stupid it was that I would have to memorize this shit. I also remember having such bad, bad grades in that class that I convinced my parents that I should go on a field trip to Wallop's Island, VA for a few days to help improve my Bio grade. Yeah, I know, it's sad that they fell for that, isn't it? I had a blast on that field trip and learned a bit about anatomy, (Heart Stomper was there, as well.) Improve my Biology grade? Not so much...

#26

Crazy is contagious.

It is; make sure your immune system is in tip-top shape.

January 27, 2010

#27

Gastro-Intestinal health should never be under-appreciated or over-estimated.

Do you *really* want me to expand on this? Just accept it and we'll all move on.

January 28, 2010

#28

Never use a bag of frozen fruit as an ice pack when you have a headache. You may think it won't leak but it will and it'll be sticky and when you try to brush your hair before you go to bed it'll only make the headache worse.

I was just putting this out there as a PSA. My effort to be thrifty and convenient backfired and then, Lacy and John weighed in.

Lacy, "I SO wanna go somewhere with the sticky idea...but I'm too classy for that."

John, "Don't act like this is the first time you're going to bed sticky."

I won't even try to follow that. ☺

#29

Although we intend to remain friends and to chat now and then, Jesus and I have agreed to see other people.

Lafayette mentioned something along these lines on *True Blood* and it struck me as both funny and insightful. I was raised Catholic and given a strong foundation in faith. I appreciate that and I won't ever consider converting to another religion because being Catholic is as much a part of who I am as having blue eyes and my love for chocolate. I am secure in my relationship with Jesus Christ but the church of man has disappointed me; as most men tend to do. However, something that has occurred to me over the past twenty years- the purpose of this little project- is that there are many, many paths to God. Jesus is one of them and we're still tight but there is certainly room in my prayer circle for a few others.

#30

Liberals and Democrats no longer shock me but they still really, really annoy me...

I'm rather political by nature and I'm generally not shy about sharing my opinion when warranted. I try not to get too political on facebook, though, because it's really just for fun. However, with the United States of America morphing into the Socialist States of America, I often find it difficult to hold my tongue.

#31

People who can solve the Rubic's cube don't get to have sex with other people. It totally works for me that I can't solve it.

I used to date this guy I call Schroeder because it amuses Lacy and me for reasons I'm not about to get into here, but I digress. He got himself all wound up about the fact that his brother could solve the Rubic's cube and he could not I dropped this little piece of truth on him when we were in bed one night. Why did I make it revelation #31? Simple, it's just me being a bitchy, self-absorbed, elitist snob. I'm okay with that because, as stated clearly above, it works for me.

20 years
Post-High School
Revelation

#32

There's a fine line between Gospel truth and gorilla shit.

Queen Sophie-Ann noted this on *True Blood* and, again, I found it amusing and thought-provoking. Much like the fine line between love and hate, what's true and what's total fabrication often are very, very similar. The older and more jaded we become, the more willing we are to believe the bullshit.

#33

Spring is six weeks away, no matter what the filthy rodent "says."

This question is for the Pennsylvania natives out there: Have you ever tried to explain Groundhog Day to a non-native? Have you ever tried to explain it to a non-American who doesn't have a firm grasp on the English language? Try it sometime, I dare you. You'll find yourself trying to justify that which is unjustifiable! Look at the calendar, people. It's six weeks away no matter what.

#34

The anticipation is always more intense than the reality.

I actually learned this when I turned thirty, but that's within the last twenty years so it counts. The weeks leading up to thirty were vile. I so did not want to be thirty! No, the alternative was no picnic, but I was about to realize the finalization of my second divorce, no kids, living back at home with my mom and I was about to be THIRTY! I woke up that morning, still single and childless in my mother's house and I was thirty. I took a shower and went to work and survived. Now, as I am playing chicken with turning forty, I keep reminding myself that it's all mental.

#35

Not so much a revelation as an "I told you so." to all my former students who had to do, or witnessed someone doing, pushups for using words like "retarded," "gay," or "faggot." Take a look at the mess Rahm Emmanual is in. You can thank me later.

For those of you reading this who have never had the experience of being a student in my class, allow me to explain. I had a long-standing rule that certain words and phrases were forbidden. Simply, anything that takes an entire group of people, lumps them together and uses that word as a negative adjective is wrong. Period. If someone is acting like an idiot, call them an idiot not a retard. If someone is being an asshole call it like you see it, don't call them gay. I put these words used as insults in the same category as ethnic or racial slurs and dumb blonde jokes. Not funny. Not acceptable. I gave my students the option of ten push-ups per infraction, to be served immediately, or sixty minutes hard-labor in detention. I hope they took away from it an understanding of the power of words. I know they had better developed pecs.

#36

Don't be a hero; take the Xanax.

Seriously, with today's pharmacology why anyone should suffer from anxiety is just beyond me. Also, I shouldn't have to suffer from your anxiety. Nobody thinks it's brave and it's sure as hell not funny. Take your shit storm far, far away from me or medicate it. Either way, it's *your* shit storm so *you* deal with it.

#37

Happiness is a pot of homemade soup on the stove and a purring kitty on your lap when there's a foot and a half of snow outside.

It was vegetable beef soup and the lap cat alternated between Ruben and Clay. ☺

#38

Everyone is entitled to be stupid but some people really abuse the privilege.

They are everywhere you go! Honestly, I think most people are simply refusing to pay attention to the world around them rather than legitimately stupid. So many are just so full of a sense of entitlement and expect the world to stop and pay attention to them that it results in truly stupid behavior. Don't they realize that this is my world and they're all just passing through? My name is *Mia*- it's all about *me*!

#39

An overwhelming number of people never really leave high school.

Okay, so I was working at an office which will remain nameless because if this book actually takes off and begins to support the lifestyle to which I would like to become accustom then I don't want to get sued. Anyway, at this office was an angry little office drone. In her defense, she was not at all attractive, not very educated and had far too many responsibilities for her pay grade. This led to a very low self-esteem and a tendency to act out in an incredibly high-schoolish manner. Being a former high school teacher, I can understand and appreciate this confluence of events that led to the poor behavior. Being paid at a rate far, far lower than that of a high school teacher and being a fellow office drone myself- I didn't give a shit. When she decided to make me her target I stood up for myself and fired back. I didn't just get mad, I got even. Please look forward to a revelation in April where the karma chameleon smiles on me.

#40

Chivalry is dead; the feminists killed it.

Later in the day, after being annoyed with the angry office drone acting out her own, personal high school drama, I read an article online about women claiming to having been offended by the superbowl commercials from the day before. Seriously? Seriously, ladies? Please get over yourselves! I am quite capable of paying my own bills and plunging the toilet. If I can't get a jar open, I improvise and if I don't have a date to an event I take a girlfriend or fly solo. That being said, I don't know how to change a tire or hang blinds and I have no intention of learning! I *love* it when a man opens the door for me, I never say no to flowers and I don't hate it when I have a strong arm to hold on to when I'm walking down Second Street at night. That being said, chivalry goes both ways. When a friend tells me he's in the hospital and not likely to leave for a while, I'm there. If I get to the door first, I hold it for the next person. It's called being polite, kind and considerate. It's about going the extra mile for the people in your life not because you expect something for it but because it makes the other person smile. Period. Gentlemen, take it from me: those nasty women claiming to be offended do NOT speak for all of us.

#41 **Women could train their hoo-has to whistle Dixie and men still want a threesome. *sigh* Silly boys...**

I've had this on-again/off-again fella for a couple of years. We don't particularly like one another "in that way" but we get along well enough and when we're both between exciting relationships we laugh, we talk about football, we watch TV and we you know... Anyway, on this particular day, we were talking and laughing, you know, and the topic of threesomes came up. Can I just tell you I have rarely seen that level of excitement in any pair of eyes outside a child on Christmas morning? For the record, before any rumors fester into facts, NO, I did not!

#42 **It snows in Pennsylvania. Shocking...**

What's the perfect follow-up to being annoyed by men craving sex with two women at the same time? Annoyance as a result of the constant "news" reporting and facebook bitching about the snow. It's February! This is Pennsylvania! IT FREAKIN' SNOWS! Can we shovel and move on now, please? There are pot holes to worry about. My brother, **Mike,** chimed in on this one, "We gotta stop this global warming thing!" Well said, brother; well said.

February 12, 2010

#43

Treating others the way you would like to be treated is fabulous in theory, bullshit in practice.

It seems that the more you are kind and generous and give people the benefit of the doubt the more they tend to take advantage of your good nature. I don't want to be a score-keeper, but there's only so many times I will go the extra step for someone before I start looking for a little consideration in return. I have this one person in my life who *only* contacts me to bitch and moan or to ask me for a favor. I've found myself not answering the phone or not responding to the text. When I get a call asking for an employment reference on her, I say I really don't know her well enough to give an honest, helpful opinion. I'm not all that worried that she'll read this and recognize herself because unless I give her a copy of this book as a gift she'll never read it.

February 13, 2010

#44

Apparently I am selfish and demanding for saying, "please call if you get stuck at work and can't make it." Wow.

I really need to take a lesson from baseball and after three strikes he is OUT. No more one more chance for the second, third, fourth and fifth time. He seriously said I was being selfish and demanding when I requested a phone call if he would be late at work. Yeah, okay. My bad for giving him so many chances. I never bothered to keep or reset the date. No, this one is not about Douche Bag. I'll call this one the Ass Hat, just to help you keep them straight.

Side Note: Ass Hat contacted me in late December. When I asked him what was new in his life, i.e. what has changed about his behavior he immediately went on the defensive. I told him to stop harassing me and ignored his next three calls. Baby steps; I'm making progress.

February 14, 2010

#45 Cupid's got some 'splainin to do. (Happy Single Awareness Day! ☺)

Is there anything that makes a single girl feel more single than Valentine's Day? Nope, didn't think so.

February 15, 2010

#46 You're never too old to play. I may be pushing 40 but I'm about to kick it like nobody's business at Bounce U, pictures to follow...

I was pretty sick during most of December and January. I won't get into details because I'm not a big fan of pity, but suffice it to say it scared the hell out of me and the people who love me. One of those people, the amazing Heather, came to my rescue when I was snowed in and unable (physically) to dig myself out. She came through in a BIG, HUGE way and there was very little I could do to thank her for it. I said thank you over and over and I gave her homemade soup but it just didn't feel like enough.

Now, Heather's a busy lady. She's got a fantastic husband who works long hours and three kids, (who are just as fabulous as she is), and a full time job AND she is a student. I decided to thank her by giving any busy, working mom what they really want and need: a day off. I took her kids for the day to Bounce U in Annville. It's a kid-gym full of those inflatable bounce house things you normally see at carnivals. It's indoor so on a snowy day off school it was perfect. We had an absolute blast and I am hoping my dear friend, Heather, knows just how much I appreciate her.

February 16, 2010

#47

The best things in life really are free. My nephew, who turns three today, has a fabulous habit of randomly saying, "Hello, gorgeous!" and "I love you," while giving the most amazing, spontaneous hugs. Priceless. Happy Birthday, Ben! Zia loves you, too. ☺

My fellow Aquarian, Ben. He gets spunkier and better looking by the minute! Be warned now, little ladies. This kid is going to break some hearts.

February 17, 2010

#48

More Americans believe that Elvis Presley is still alive than believe that Pres. Obama's economic programs have created jobs. It's not really a revelation, but damn it made me laugh. ☺

Yeah, I said I'm a little political on facebook sometimes...

#49

The only constant is change.

Remember when I was pontificating on the anticipation being more intense than the reality? Yeah, I wrote this one the day before my birthday. Still nursing a little bit of left over bummed-out feeling over Douche Bag but trying to remind myself that there is something better waiting for me.

#50

Although, like a fine wine, I am getting better with age it's taking me a long time to become the woman I want to be.

And we have arrived at my thirty-eighth birthday. Better than I was but still miles from where I want to be. It's good to have goals, though. Imagine how boring life would be if we had nothing left to learn?

#51

When I appreciate what I have rather than lamenting what I want, the Universe gives me what I need. Thank you, all, for the birthday wishes, texts, calls, drinks, hugs & kisses! From Happy Hour at the Fire House to Playland at McDonald's and all points in between, you made turning 38 painless and fabulous!!

I could have spent the day turning thirty-eight lamenting the fact that I am single and childless but instead I embraced what was all around me. I have *fabulous* friends, *fantastic* family and a *flawless* ability to find joy and laughter everywhere I go. Life is good.

February 21, 2010

#52
You need to wipe your own ass; my hands are full.

Still riding my birthday high, a little PSA to all those unwilling to take care of their own issues.

February 22, 2010

#53
Hockey Rocks! (yes, I know this is not news to many of you, but I have become a fan since teaching at CC ☺) Way to go Team USA!!

I love the Olympics. Seriously. I *love* them. Maybe it's because my dad loved them, maybe it's because I'm fiercely patriotic or maybe it's because I love competition. I don't know, whatever combination it is I freakin' *love* the Olympics! Summer, winter, trials- bring it on. This revelation was born from watching Team USA kick hockey ass in Canada.

February 23, 2010

#54
Never underestimate the healing powers of a good night's sleep and a hot shower.

I went to bed with Prince NyQuil the night before. After quite a busy weekend I could not sell a cold at work, even if it was true. Knock-out cold meds led to a deep sleep and a hot shower brought me back to full capacity. Cold be gone!

#55
When determination, strength & grace collide beauty is born; and anything is possible.

Do you remember the story of Canadian figure skater Joannie Rochette? Her mother died unexpectedly in the morning and that night she went on to skate in the Olympics. It was the bravest, most beautiful performance I've ever seen, (let's review my Olympic obsession, shall we?) It was truly a study in the triumph of the human spirit. You took my breath away, Joannie! Thank you for showing the entire world just what women are capable of even under the most horrendous of circumstance.

#56
Bon Jovi was absolutely right, we are all just livin' on a prayer; so we've got to hold on to what we've got. It doesn't make a difference if we'll make it or not. We've got each other, and that's a lot, for love; we'll give it a shot.

Every now and then, one of my revelations really struck a chord and the comments I received were fantastic. I either just had my finger on the pulse of the public-at-large or we were all fooling around at work. Whatever, this one was one of those really fun ones.

John, "He accused me of giving love a bad name once."

Mia, "Were you shot through the heart?"

John, "Yes, but I was wanted Dead or Alive for Living in Sin."

Mia, "Man, that's just bad medicine."

John, "to cure my Social Disease?"

Mia, "Oh my, that night you looked in the mirror and asked, You Wanna Make a Memory, didn't you? Be careful what you wish for, buddy!"

Jody, "Oh boy, I think you both need a ticket to destination anywhere … east or west, I don't care!"

Mia, "Are you suggesting we Runaway?"

John, "we'll go to Dry County and get Wild in the Streets!"

Jody, "yes! … and don't forget to send postcards from the wasteland"

Mia, "I'll take the Homebound Train. John?"

Jody, "And do it all a thousand times again … no regrets?"

Mia, "Sure, why not? Who says you can't go home?"

John, "Joey, but he's Misunderstood."

Mia, "Don't worry, John. I'll Be There For You."

John, "Thank You for Loving Me."

Mia, "It's the least I can do, I really appreciate the way you Lay Your Hands on Me."

John, "I'm All About Lovin' You!"

Mia, "Even in a Bed of Roses?"

John, "Everyday! So Get Ready, because I'm Burning for Love and you better be Open All Night!"

Jody, "Ya know ... I drove all night down streets that wouldn`t bend, but somehow they drove me back here once again!"

Mia, "You're going down in a Blaze of Glory, Jody!"

Jody, "Well Mia, Someday all the boys are gonna find out that you won`t even play it with them...You're running out of numbers baby!"

Mia, "Just Blame it on the Love of Rock & Roll!"

Jody, "so you guys Dressed up just like ziggy but he couldn't play guitar ... Captain crash (John) and the beauty queen (Mia) from mars!"

John, "We win at the Internet. Well played."

Jody, "whew ... I didn't realize they had so many songs! ☺"

Mia, "That was the most fun I've had with my clothes on in a long time! Thanks for playing. ☺"

February 26, 2010

#57 Even if you're in a borrowed car, driving past his house just to see if he's home is stalker behavior. just sayin'

No, really, I'm just sayin'...

#58
You can't recognize happiness if you never know heartache.

I hesitated to actually explain this one because I'm not as pathetic as it's about to seem. This was written on Douche Bag's birthday. He did not break my heart. I ended things with him before I fell in love with him. I *was* very disappointed that things didn't work out and I was even more disappointed that he didn't come chasing after me after I dumped him. Fellas, don't you know that's pretty much the only reason we push you away? duh...

Anyway, I was getting ready to go to away on a little mini vacation the next day with another man and just like my first wedding when I was waiting for Heart Stomper to stop me from saying "I do" I guess I was waiting for Douche Bag to stop me from getting on that plane. I didn't want to come right out on facebook and say *that* so I dug a little deeper into the real, actual heartache I know all too well and wrote this revelation.

Douche Bag, if you're reading this, damn did you ever blow a chance at a great thing between you and me.

#59
If you can't be with the one you want, want the one you're with? Not so sure I believe it, but it's a theory well worth testing as I sit here in the airport about to do just that.

Big surprise that yesterday's revelation failed to get the attention I had hoped for from Douche Bag. Actually, I wasn't all that surprised as he had been quite silent ever since I stopped seeing him. It was during this post-break up period that I spontaneously accepted an invitation to go to Las Vegas with a man I dated briefly when I was deployed to Minnesota for the

2008 Senate recount. Nice guy, nothing bad I can say about him, just maybe not the one for me. He knew this when he offered to take me along and despite my protests, *bing* a plane ticket pops up in my email. So I sat in the airport wishing Douche Bag hadn't turned out to be such a douche bag, trying to get myself psyched up for a little mini vacay in Las Vegas. I'll sum it up for you: glad I went, theory is bullshit.

Fun Fact: Heart Stomper was quite concerned about my travel companion and became convinced that I was about to make national news by ending up disemboweled in a Vegas hotel room. Ergo, he put himself on standby to come rescue me. Where the fuck was that attitude on January 4, 1992?

Another Fun Fact: The fabulous Heather posted on Douche Bag's wall, "Happy Belated birthday. Wish you could have spent it with that someone special but she's in Vegas. Hope you had a good one."

Yes, I know it was childish and immature but hot damn, it was funny!

20 years
Post-High School
Revelation

#60

We're all responsible for our own amusement; entertain yourself.

Okay, so I was in Vegas with a man I really did not want to be with and still partially wishing that Douche Bag wasn't a douche bag when it occurred to me that I can't keep looking for a man to gauge my happiness on. I need to be happy with *me*. I was having this fabulous, girl-power epiphany when a couple of my facebook friends chimed in.

Lacy, "Wow, I wanna go with something about masturbation there but it's still early on a Monday."

Greg, "Lacy beat me to it- no pun intended."

Fun Fact: Greg was the first boy I ever "slept" with. We were three or four-years-old. One of our moms covered us with the same blanket. Scandalous. ☺

#61

I had the revelation here in Vegas; ergo it's staying here...

It was a good one, too.

March 3, 2010

#62

The handicapped, extra-large stall, a travel pack of baby wipes, fresh panties and clean socks will do in a pinch but what airports really need are shower facilities. There is money to be made there. Seriously.

Ever have delayed and cancelled flights and end up living in the airport for a day or two? Yeah, snow in Jersey meant no connecting flight and the thought of going back to the hotel with Minnesota Man was no bueno. I set up camp at the airport and found cleanliness where I could.

#63

March 4, 2010

There's no place like home. ☺

#64

March 5, 2010

Bliss is not having the best of everything; it's making the best of everything I have.

I have some really fantastic things and people in my life and I sometimes forget to appreciate them when I'm yearning for more.

#65

An hour's worth of fresh air and sunshine washes away a week's worth of drama and stress!

Here we arrive at the Saturday after my trip tentative to and arduous trip home from Las Vegas. I took my aunt's dog for a nice, long walk and all was once again right with the world.

#66

Pedicure+Red Polish=Happy Feet. ☺

There's really something wrong with the people out there that don't like to have their feet touched. Damn, I love it. Foot massage, pedicure, pampering? It really helps me get in touch with my inner-princess. She's far too often stifled by the realities of life; what with all the working and bill-paying and responsibilities. Please...

#67

Every new beginning comes from some other beginning's end. (yeah, I know that's from a song; doesn't make it any less true!)

Not sure, but I think I was still stuck on stupid over Douche Bag and desperately trying to force myself out of it. It must have worked because I can't remember exactly why I chose this revelation on this particular day! And don't give me any shit about still being stuck, at least I have the balls to be honest about my tendency to obsess about and to try to fix that which is beyond my control.

#68

The world can be divided into two groups; those who step up & face their fears and those who run & hide. Which are you?

I wrote today's revelation after thinking about a bumper sticker I used to pass frequently when I was walking in beautiful, downtown Lemoyne. The sticker read, "Are you going to cowboy up or just lay there and bleed?" I always chuckled at it and decided to paraphrase a bit. For the record: I'm a face your fears kinda gal.

#69

I've got balls bigger than most men; sadly, that includes most of the men I've dated.

With this revelation being #69, my inner-frat boy demanded something with the word "balls" in it. My facebook friends took it and really ran with it.

Tom, "You see! That's what I'm talkin about Mia! Now that's a revelation. PS we were all afraid of you then and revere you now ☺"

Mia, "Thanks, Tommy! ☺ You were afraid of me? Why? I don't bite...hard..."

Jeff, "Tom always bit when he was wrestling..."

Mia, "Damn, I should have joined the wrestling team."

#70

It's never too late to do the right thing, apologize, ask for a second chance or to choose happiness.

Hey, remember Heart Stomper? I told you a little about him. Yeah, eighteen years later he found me, called me and apologized for stomping on my heart. It didn't happen the day I wrote this but he and I have been communicating periodically since then. He'll turn up again in our little story. Stay tuned.

#71

WORDS ARE CHEAP. It's not enough to say you care, you must actually DO something about it. That's why I just registered for the 3-day/60 miles walk to raise money for Breast Cancer Research. Will you put a few dollars up for your love and appreciation of the Boobies? Check out the box on my page- on the left.

I registered for the Susan G. Komen 3-day walk to support Breast Cancer Research and went on to raise a pile of money only to be denied the opportunity to walk because I changed jobs and my insurance lapsed. ☹ But, on a positive note, I've registered to walk October 14-16 in Philadelphia! I'll be hitting up everyone I know for money, again, and I really love my job so I don't anticipate any problems with a lapse in insurance. Please, help me save second base and donate here: http://www.the3day.org

#72

The Hokey Pokey really *IS* what it's all about!

Seriously, put your whole self in or take your whole self out, shake it all about. Do the Hokey Pokey and turn yourself around. ***That's*** what it's all about!

#73

The moment you settle for less than what you're worth you begin to get exactly what you deserve.

Honestly, I can know this but still struggle to live it. I am the queen of making excuses and allowances and trying to see the other side and blah, blah, blah. I really do need to walk the walk and not just talk the talk. *sigh*

#74

Sometimes the best words of comfort and advice are the ones you simply listen to when spoken by the friend in pain.

Okay, to explain this one it may seem I'm just blowing sunshine up my own ass but I'm really not. Honestly, this was a real light-bulb moment for me. I was having coffee with a friend of mine the day before and she was having a real time of it. Between school, men, family and battling personal demons she was feeling like she was being pulled in a million directions. I *wanted* to say something helpful, I *wanted* to have some pearls of wisdom, some words of advice, and I had nothing. Instead, I just listened. I really, truly *listened* to her and didn't try to solve anything or encapsulate it or stuff it into a cute little phrase. I just listened. We cried. She felt better. Did I solve any of her problems? Hell no. However, she knew she wasn't alone and I think that was the best I could offer her on that day. She has no idea the valuable lesson she taught me. Thanks, chica!

March 16, 2010

#75

Blonde is more than a hair color; it's a lifestyle choice.

psh, you know it's true.

March 17, 2010

#76

Giving medication to a cat can be an entertaining proposition. (credit Dr. Sean and my lucky Irish lass of a friend, Beth, for making this revelation possible.)

Here's the story, of my friend named Bethie, she was bringing up two lovely Siamese. And the story, of her honey, Jason, who was busy with two shelter cats of his own. Yeah, you may *think* you know how the rest of this story goes…think again! Beth's cats and Jason's cats did not react to their parents' cohabitation as well as one would hope. In fact, they reacted so badly that it was decided to attempt to put Oliver on a little kitty-prozac. Oy to the vey! Talk about Oliver Stoned.

This wasn't just a case of some over-zealous hissing. Oliver would stalk Bailey in the litter box. Now come on, if the poor cat can't even take a pleasant shit then something's got to give. Oliver being the biggest instigator and certainly the bully of the house, he was the first to make a visit to the doctor to see what could be done. After all was said and done, Jason and Beth decided to simply keep their cats separated. They just said no to drugs.

March 18, 2010

#77

A well-lived life leaves a little chaos in its wake; if you don't have dirt under your nails from time to time you're missing something.

I've long held to the theory that I've been an active participant in my life; not a spectator. I highly recommend it.

March 19, 2010

#78

Outside of a dog, a book is man's best friend. Inside of a dog it's too dark to read.

I read this somewhere and it cracked me up!

March 20, 2010

#79

Always look both ways and hold a grown-up's hand when you cross the street. (It's really Ben's revelation, but it's a good one anyway.)

I don't remember why I was taking care of my nephew that day, but for some reason it was just the two of us and he hit me with that little tidbit. Now, before you get all Judgy Judgmental on me, I would *never* have let him cross the street without holding my hand- he had just turned three! However, he dropped this little bomb of insight on me as we were each reaching for the other's hand and it struck me that this is really, really good advice at thirty-eight, too. The hand becomes more figurative than literal and the looking both ways is not just to scope out traffic. Know what's coming at you from all directions and have a good support system in place, surround yourself with people smarter than you are and you'll be okay out there in the middle of the road.

March 21, 2010

#80

It's okay to indulge your addictive personality and extremely competitive nature if it's for a good cause.

You want to argue with me on this one? I'll race you for it. My sister and I were in a fierce battle to see who could raise our money for the Boobie Walk faster. Good times. ☺

March 22, 2010

#81

Charming is just an asshole who smiles.

I don't mind charming, I can be very charming. I just know better than to confuse charming for genuine emotion. Charming makes you laugh and blush and, if you're lucky, charming will make your toes curl. However, charming is a surface-only kind of thing. It's okay to be charming just please be packing more than that if you expect to stick around for a while.

#82

Intimidation is in the eye of the beholder.

Pardon me while I unleash a little bit with a rant. I've been told more than a few times that I am very intimidating. Apparently, I am supposed to be ashamed of this. I am supposed to then alter my behavior to be less intimidating. You know what? Bite me. Bite me now or make an appointment for later and I'll see what I can do to pencil you in. You find me intimidating? That's your freakin' problem! Grow a set and get over it; put on your big girl panties and be a worthy opponent. Don't expect me to back down because you are intimidated by me. When you tell me that you expose your jugular, you silly twit! There's your first lesson in having a spine: never let someone know that you feel unworthy. If you do, then you are.

/end rant

#83

While the "experts" are sitting around debating how & why, I've found if I just get started I accomplish the task quite well.

I remember this one quite well and it also involves that angry little office drone I told you about back in #39. There was this hideously boring meeting about how to improve organization and paper flow at our office. It was so pointless; it was really just an exercise in figuring out how to assign blame for whatever was going wrong at any given time. The hour wasted in that meeting was an hour I did not get to spend actually focusing on the paper problem. When the meeting was over, resolving only to have another meeting to presumably go over all the same shit again, I just went back to my office and did it my way. It got done, the information was accessible and we were well-within compliance. Quit talking about it and just do it already. God, I love Nike.

#84

March 25, 2010

If it says new and improved, it's probably bullshit.

Don't say I didn't warn you.

#85

March 26, 2010

Sarcasm is the body's natural defense mechanism against others' stupidity.

I have to give credit to a childhood friend, Heather, for this revelation. She had it posted the day before as her status and I thought it was *brilliant*! A few of my facebook friends thought so, too.

Ted, "Keep your immune systems strong, ladies. There is an epidemic out there lately."

Patty, "you're posting an awful lot about sarcasm lately..."

Mia, "I've been in the presence of a lot of stupidity lately..."

Just so you know, I'm fluent in sarcasm.

#86

Never underestimate the power of boobies.

It's true; they open doors and start conversations but they can also kill. I was working overtime trying to raise money for the 3-day walk and was posting a lot to encourage donations. Some choice comments:

Andrea, "Every woman should tattoo that sentence to the inside of her eyelids. Although, I'm most impressed with the women who, having lost their boobies, draw strength from their fellow females to fight for a cure for breast cancer...two kick-ass sisters come to mind. ☺"

Jeff, "Deadly weapons they can be."

John, "Never have, never will. If I had back all the time and money I spent trying to get to touch them I'd be a four-year-old millionaire."

#87

I didn't post a revelation yesterday and although the world didn't end, I felt all sorts of guilt for breaking my commitment to the project. Wings and beer helped me get over it, but still. I am a lot more dedicated to my word than I used to be. Go figure.

This was more than a revelation for me; it was an epiphany. I had decided I would write a revelation every day and on that particular Sunday I just didn't. I went out for wings with friends, I probably did some laundry, but I didn't post a revelation. It really bothered me to drop the ball like that. I was amazed at my personal censure and rather proud. It's a hint that I'm actually becoming the person I want to be.

March 29, 2010

#88

Always go up hill on the first half of the walk.

This was one of those rare days that I made two revelations in one day. I was able to double up because I had skipped the day before and it was another epiphany made in real time while training for the 3-day walk. Oy.

March 30, 2010

#89

I am a morning person- and I refuse to apologize for it!

You know what else I will not apologize for? I hate peanut butter! I'm not allergic to it, but I tell people I am because I don't want to hear them say, "You don't like peanut butter?! What's wrong with you?" Nothing. I just don't like peanut butter. Or barbecue sauce or ketchup. And I like to be just slightly chilly, not hot. And I don't like to sit in a car with the seat tipped back so I feel like an astronaut. And I like my water room temperature. And I like both cats and dogs. And I enjoy waking up early and getting a jump start on the day. I'm a morning person; get over it.

#90

The longest journey begins with a single step. I've walked 97.4 miles in the last 19 days to train for the Boobie March! Please support me with a donation- quick & easy; link is on my wall. If each of my fb friends gives just $5 I'll pass my goal. Many thanks to those who have already donated & thanks to those who will give up just one Starbucks to save a life.

More boobie begging. ☺ At some point in my Boobie Begging Bonanza, I wrote this fun, little ditty:

This little Boobie went to market,
This little Boobie stayed home.
This little Boobie had cancer,
This little Boobie had none.
Together, we can make sure that no little Boobies have to cry,
"Why me? Why me?" ever again!

Oh come on, you know you grinned a little.

20 years
Post-High School
Revelation

#91

When you take care of you, you're much better able to take care of others.

You know when you're on a plane and you're trying to ignore the flight attendants going through their little schpiel about seatbelts and emergency exits but you can't because you're pre-occupied with thinking, "Who the fuck doesn't know how to buckle a seat belt and why must they all use two fingers to point?" Yeah, well, they also always tell you to put on your own oxygen mask before you help someone else with theirs. It's good advice. Also good advice, take a shower and wear non-scented deodorant before you get into the same cabin as me, please. Thanks.

#92

Perception is indeed reality; do you see a rose bush full of thorns or a thorn bush that has sprouted roses?

If you find yourself saying, "What I meant when I said that is…" more than once a month then you've got yourself a little perception problem. You should work on that.

#93

Workmen on the roof at 7:30 on a Saturday morning sucks; big time.

A couple of my Outlaw friends pointed out that if the workmen were really hot and happened to fall through the roof and, literally, into my lap I wouldn't mind so much. Good theory, but the truth of the matter is that I was in bed and what with the bed head, morning breath and most likely presence of more body hair than I usually like to sprout, did I really want company at that moment? Not so much...

#94 Never exchange what you want the most for what you want in the moment.

A little Weight Watcher's tip that lends itself well to all aspects of life.

#95 Oprah has lots of a-ha moments; I need her to have one while reading one of my books. Who's going to help me make that happen?

If you're reading this then you're no doubt aware that I've written a few books. My following is small, but dedicated, and they would really like me to get off my ass and write some more. I would like that too but I need either a sugar daddy or a big, mainstream publishing break. At this step in my life's journey I could go either way.

#96

I no longer fight the winds of change. Instead, I spread my wings and fly into the next adventure.

I had taken the day off work the day before- migraines, they're not just for breakfast anymore. Anyhoo, one of the girls at work had put in her two weeks' notice and I emailed the boss that night when the grapevine got around to me. When I came into work the next morning, I was called into a meeting which turned into another meeting which turned into an interview for that evening after work. I had only been at the company for a little over three months and I knew nothing about the position for which I was applying but I thought, "Screw it, I'm going for it." I'm not going to resist something new just because it's new. Maybe it'll be the best thing ever! This is the theory that has led to many a disaster. just sayin'

#97

Boneless hot wings are really just chicken nuggets with delusions of grandeur.

LOL, sometimes I crack myself up.

#98

I must learn patience. Now!

I wrote this when I was being cryptic while waiting to hear if I'd gotten the promotion at work I'd been interviewing for. I was waiting, and waiting, and waiting and I'm not very good at that.

Ted, "You'll get it. Give it time. ☺"

Yeah, that was no help; although it did make me laugh. By this point I was on my third interview in as many days and to add insult to injury that angry little office drone was also vying for the job. I could handle not getting it because, quite frankly, I didn't have the experience or seniority, but Oh.My.God I would rather eat my fist than have my arch-nemesis get it!

April 9, 2010

#99   **Indeed, good things DO come to those who wait!**

I got the promotion! I had to wait until 4:30 on Friday afternoon to find out but I was so grateful that I didn't have to sweat it out over the weekend. And my arch-nemesis was now below me on the corporate hierarchy… WOOT!

April 10, 2010

#100   **To earn an animal's love and trust is to earn mine. Happy 7th birthday to my beautiful boys: Ruben & Clay.**

In November 2002 I had to say goodbye to my loyal friend and fierce protector; my German Shepherd, Peyton. She was almost eleven and had lived a good long life. Two husbands came and went, but Peyton was always there to love me no matter what kind of mood I was in. It was about six months after she died that I thought I was ready to have another pet but I just couldn't bring myself to get another dog. A student of mine at that time told me that her cat had just had kittens. I went to meet the kittens and fell ass over teacups in love with these two little boys.

They were tiny little things; together they weighed just one pound. One was black and the other ginger-striped. Pairs of names were considered and discarded. I liked Ben & Jerry because I loved the ice cream but they never responded to it. I thought about Bill & Ted but I had students called "Bill" and "Ted" in class that semester and I thought that would be awkward. Bill is now known as Will and I've lost touch with Ted so maybe it wouldn't have been so awkward after all. Ponderous. I *really* wanted to name them Don Pedro and John the Bastard because they are the brothers in my favorite Shakespearean comedy, *Much Ado About Nothing,* but could you imagine me standing on the porch calling for them to come in the house? Okay, you probably can, but still; not the best choice.

I brought them home on May 19, 2003; the night of the *American Idol* finale. I looked at them and I looked at the TV. And then back at them. Ruben Studdard Semuta and Clayton Aiken Semuta owned me from the get go. They've grown into their names. Ruben went from being so tiny that he had to be bottle fed to being chubby and quite vocal when he wants to be, (he's the black one.) And Clay? Oh, Clay is *fabulous*! He's got lovely blonde and gold highlights in his ginger-hair and boyfriend loves his pedicures. My boys. Mamma loves you!

#101 *April 11, 2010*
All work and no play sucks.

I was so excited about the promotion and sticking it to my arch-nemesis that I glossed over the fact that no one had been hired to replace me in my current position. I was due to start training the next day so into the office I went on a Sunday to try and get a jump the pile of work on my old desk before I tackle a new desk. Damn that sense of responsibility I developed and discussed back in #87. It snatched my lazy Sunday right out of my hands.

April 12, 2010

#102

If you think you can do something or not; you're right.

First day on the new job, wrote this one as both an homage to Henry Ford who first said it and also to psych myself up for the task at hand. I could not wait to see the look on arch-nemesis' face! (I know that's very shallow of me but give me a break, I'm a work in progress.)

April 13, 2010

#103

Revenge may well be best served cold but vindication tastes great piping hot, room temperature, chilled or frozen solid. ☺

Angry office drone / arch-nemesis was not at work on Monday. She called off. Why? Why you ask? Nobody knows for sure but that didn't make my moment any less bright when she had to come into MY office for the morning meeting. HA! Chew on that, rat face! (Would very much appreciate that break, please; still a work in progress.)

#104

I love the end result but I do not enjoy the learning process.

So, still loving that I got the promotion but accepting the reality that I really do not know what I am doing.

#105

April 15, 2010

Good friends are hard to find; it's best to just let the Universe put them in your path.

In the face of being clueless at my new job the best thing to do is bitch up storm on the phone with one friend on your way over to drink wine and have dinner at another friend's house. Now, Kelly is my best friend, I claimed her in the name of Mia back in 1986 and Beth is a relatively new friend- just about a year- but the Universe really knew what it was doing when they each landed in my path. ♥ Kelly provides the calm sense of reason I need and Beth lets me get all wound up and talk a lot of shit. My yin and my yang. Thanks, girls! Funny how facebook felt strongly about this, too.

Kelly, "a very wise person must have been mentoring you for 25 yrs ☺"

Mia, "It's true, Kelly- the Universe put a fabulous person in my English class in 9th grade and I'm a far better person for it. ☺"

Beth, "@Mia - I couldn't agree more! You are the Baileys in my coffee!"

Tom, "Good friends come from your past not your future. Many of us in our later 30's early 40's either have good friends or we burn through people in which case we really don't. I for one am very fortunate with the relationships I have built in my life and I am at quota with good friends. The rest of the world albeit most good people that deserve kindness are just riders on the train."

Just for the record, Tom would have been there helping to put the shattered pieces of Mia back together that night if I had called him. It turns out Kelly and Beth did the trick. So well, in fact, that I wrote the next day's revelation at dinner that night…

April 16, 2010

#106

Gin makes me cry, wine makes me giggle, rum makes me dance but tequila makes me talk dirty in Spanish. ☺

Aye carumba! There was a claim by one commenter that he's heard me do this in English as well, but I'm still re-thinking our friendship since REM-gate. Chad, you're suspect.

April 17, 2010

#107

It's not enough to just say "thank you." True gratitude manifests in our actions, thoughts, intentions AND words.

I try to live this one every day. I try.

April 18, 2010

#108

Sunday is no longer a day of rest but rather a day of get the rest of your shit done because it all starts all over again tomorrow!

Yet another weekend spent at my office trying to finish up the old job and get a grip on the new one. At this point, it's not going very well.

April 19, 2010

#109

I am wise and worldly about so much and yet still oh so naïve about so much more.

My first day on the new job flying solo and I realize that my predecessor who had "trained" me failed to mention several key details and it seemed that she purposely gave me false information on a few others. Okay, so that's how we're going to play this? I think I'll just put my head down on my desk and cry now.

April 20, 2010

#120

A little meltdown now and then is good for the soul.

No, really, I put my head down on my desk and cried the day before. But, I woke up on *this* day determined to make it work. I did. ☺

#111

I still suck at math; yesterday's revelation was only #110...d'oh!

True story. FYI, the new job I was so struggling with did not in involve math.

#112

The only true motivation to actually get out of bed is a full bladder.

I actually thought of this one while I was laying in bed that morning thinking how I'd like to just call off work and not get out of bed all day but since I had to get up to pee anyway I might as well take a shower and since I'm clean and all, clothes wouldn't be out of the question and hell, I'm dressed, I guess I'll go to work...

#113

To honor the Bard is not so hard; Simply make a rhyme, as you have the time; to honor his birthday, in a couplet sort of way. Happy Birthday, William Shakespeare!

Have you caught on to the fact yet that I love Shakespeare? Some of my facebook friends do, too.

Donna, "If you read all his plays; It would take many days."

Kathy, "Your bosses may lurk, for those still at work... to be fired would be vexing, because you are texting."

Kelly, "To have a heart mend takes a best friend, to be by your side and there to confide, to laugh and cry thru the lows and the high, you play that role and you're part of my soul. Love you!"

Mia, "@Donna, so true! @Aunt Kathy, so funny!! @Kelly, so not fair! You make me choke up; love you, too, Bestie. ❤"

Michael, "a rose by any other name.....that was part of our weekly quote today, you have to love his wit and humor and realistic approach to writing. Hamlet is one of my all time faves, from me it gets all of the raves."

April 24, 2010

#114 I can WANT to scratch somebody's eyes out and yet resist the urge to do so. I call this maturity. ☺

Let me just tell you that the angry little office drone picked one hell of a day to be a pain in my ass. So you're upset that I got the promotion and you didn't? Boo-fucking-hoo. And I'm actually starting to get the hang of it, too? Somebody call the WAAHHMBULANCE! Today would have been my eleventh wedding anniversary but somebody else is married to my husband- things are rough all over.

No, not Rebound. He was my first husband. I'm talking about Kermit. I'll sum it up real quick for you. I loved him and wanted to have babies. He said he loved me, but I think he loved himself more and he moved out of the house while I was at work one day. Can I just tell you how much *that* sucked? I had to go to work every day and hear the kids call me "Mrs." Knowing full well there was no "Mr." at home. I got to keep the dog, though; it wasn't a total loss.

#115

There are three sides to every story; his, hers and the truth.

My friend, Cristina, said this to me once way back in the day when we were living in Kansas. I think I had gotten over Heart Stomper by then but I was still trying to find a way out of my marriage to Rebound. There were also a few of my favorite mistakes thrown into the mix when she dropped this golden nugget of wisdom on me.

#116

Naps freakin' rule!

Apparently, I was sleepy.

#117

Vick's Vapor Rub and a good nap is as good as a magic wand.

Sleepy and congested; come on, they can't all be great. YOU try coming up with something clever every fuckin' day.

#118

Time keeps on slippin', slippin, slippin' into the future...

Do you think Steve Miller intended to be all insightful when he wrote that song? Or was he just high and couldn't think of anything else? Whatever, dude, I'm with you. I want to fly like an eagle, too.

April 29, 2010

#119 **Exhaustion, following a job well-done, is total satisfaction.**

The good news: at this point I was getting a grip on the new job. I damn well should as I was working a ridiculous amount of hours!

April 30, 2010

#120 **Every single day I discover something new about who I am or what I am capable of.**

Oh, look at that. The Mia we all know and, (usually), love is back. The confidence bucket is full, baby! I had a strong grasp on the new job and I'd just moved into my new house. Life was good.

20 years
Post-High School
Revelation

#121

No amount is too high a price to pay for peace.

The month of May makes me think of war and peace, love and loss.

#122

One night in Bangkok makes a hard man humble.

And sometimes I just hear a song that strikes me as intriguing. ☺ My friend, **Rob,** likes to push the envelope, "- and a humble man...?" I'll let you all finish that one on your own.

#123

Today I am simply satisfied with having used what I learned instead of feeling stressed for having learned nothing new.

This was a Monday and I really had my sea legs with the new job. That day, I found myself actually knowing what I was doing and decided to give myself a pass for not having added to the knowledge base.

May 4, 2010

#124

Definition of SUCKS: waking up 2.5 hours before the alarm and just falling back to sleep 15 minutes before it goes off!

May 5, 2010

#125

A vagina is a very hostile environment. Don't say I didn't warn you.

Okay, friends, cue the heart-wrenching, tense music that would accompany the clip they play at the Oscars ceremony when introducing the nominee for Best Actress. This revelation was born during a visit to my OBGYN. The fellas out there may want to turn away now...

A vagina *is* a hostile environment and mine particularly so. Apparently, I've wanted to have a baby so badly for so long that my hoo-ha decided to kick things up a notch in the 'ol fuck you game. I grew a tumor to fill the void in my uterus. Allow me to re-iterate my penchant for doing nothing half-assed. While having an internal ultrasound, (if you're familiar then you understand my discomfort; if you're not familiar go be blissful in your ignorance), the doctor says, "Wow! That's huge!" ummm, yeah, hi; not really what a girl wants to hear when she's all up in the stirrups and already suffering from a little over-zealous waxing.

Long story short: my options were a hysterectomy- which would throw a real monkey wrench in my baby quest- or surgery to remove the tumor which may or may not be malignant. I opted for the tumor removal. It wasn't going to be pleasant either way, but at least we knew why I was so sick in the winter. More on that later.

May 6, 2010

#126

Take the *Glee* Soundtrack with half a Xanax and wash it down with a cup of Parisian Almond Crème coffee and you've got a recipe for brilliance.

Ahhh, the glorious combination of health problems and a stressful job. Thank God for pharmaceuticals.

May 7, 2010

#127

I refuse to apologize if I have done nothing wrong because I'M NOT SORRY!!

Women apologize far too much. Seriously. If I've done something wrong, intentionally or not, I'll apologize and I'll mean it. If I haven't, I'm not saying it. Forget it. Can't make me do it. And I'm not sorry about it, either.

May 8, 2010

#128

I can still rock a scrunchie like nobody's business!

Megan, "The question isn't whether you CAN...it's whether you SHOULD!"

Mia, "Et tu, Megan?"

Megan, "Haha. Pehaps we need to rewatch the *Sex and the City* 'scrunchie' episode. ☺"

Mia, "Beth- did you put her up to this? It keeps my hair out of my face and doesn't break my hair. I LOVE A SCRUNCHIE!!!"

Stephanie, "Speechless... First that you wore one, then you actually, in print, justified its use..."

Mia, "I will not be shamed; I will wear my scrunchies with pride no matter what any sisters, friends, friends-of-sisters or fictional-characters-who-wear-tastefully-questionable-ensembles have to say!!"

Todra, "There are support groups to help you stop that."

Donna, "Mia you look awesome whatever you wear. Wear whatever you like."

Christie, "my mom bought me a scrunchie for my birthday..."

Beth, "You keep telling yourself that, Mia! I'll turn your ass in to *What Not To Wear* like nobody's business!"

Todra, "Wow. Beth is ruthless. I only wanted to get you into a support group."

Lacy, "We are sisters of the scrunchie, Mia. Don't let peer pressure get you down."

Mia, "Go ahead, keep on hatin'! I'm about to begin scrunchie day, the sequel; just as soon as I get out of bed!"

Todra, "Okay, I see this is serious. You have no intention of repenting. It's time for an intervention."

Beth, "Mia - I encourage you to "rock" whatever you want in your hair; however, if you see Clinton or Stacey...don't run!"

Mia, "Due to the clear and present danger my friends and family have displayed to their well-being, my scrunchies and banana clips are now in protective custody. Oh, I'll still wear them but I no longer feel secure leaving them unattended in their cozy, sink-side basket."

Fun Fact: I am wearing a scrunchie *right now* as I write this! ☺

May 9, 2010

#129

You don't have to grow your children under your heart to be a mom; they can grow in it. Whether your kids have 2 legs or 4, call you Mommy, Zia, Gramma, teacher or friend- Happy Mother's Day! ❤

I have children; lots and lots of them. It just so happens that other women have born them and kindly loaned them to me to love and care for. Of course I'm a mom to Ruben, Clay and I'm a mom to my angels in heaven: Peyton, Abby, Callie, Sam, Benny, Buttons, the list goes on. Mothering, true mothering, is not a biological function but a conscious choice made in love.

#130

May 10, 2010

I am a stickler for crevice cleanliness.

I think the whole world is better off that I don't remember why I was compelled to celebrate hygiene.

#131

May 11, 2010

I still don't know the wing span of an unladen swallow...

I freakin' love Monty Python.

#132

May 12, 2010

It's a damn good thing that I can't actually give back all my tomorrows for just one more yesterday because I totally would.

Remember when I said that May makes me think of war and peace, love and loss? Yeah, it does.

#133

May 13, 2010

You can't win if you don't play.

I'm not just talkin' lottery, here. You have to put yourself out there, take a chance, send the text- even if he once stomped on your heart. Carpe Diem, bitches!

#134

May 14, 2010

Into every life a little rain must fall but it SUCKS when you're at the park with the kids!!

This one was fairly literal. I had Averi, Abby, Bubba and Ben for the afternoon/evening and we were at the park when va-

va-va-VOOM lighting struck and the downpour happened. There was shelter to be had under the gazebo and duck, duck goose to be played, but still. You couldn't wait another three or four hours, Mother Nature? Sheesh...

May 15, 2010

#135

The will of God won't take you to any place where the grace of God can't protect you.

I'm sure you've heard the adage, "whatever doesn't kill you makes you stronger." I believe that to be true and, frankly, I'm damn-near immortal at this point. However, it's a little more negative than I was willing to let myself be on this particular date in history. I remember reading that phrase somewhere and I wish I could remember where to give proper credit, but it was so poignant to me that I had to use it anyway. I have to hold on to the belief that God's will has a purpose and His protection is flawless. Even if it means we have to say goodbye to someone we love or even die ourselves to fulfill His purpose, His love and light will keep us close and safe and ease the transition. Not an easy lesson to learn, but certainly well-worth it in the end.

May 16, 2010

#136

Not everything that is broken can be mended with glue or tape.

Some broken things, like hearts, can never be made whole again. They can be made to function again but the scar remains.

#137

May 17, 2010

Although I've learned a lot about myself and the world around me, I still struggle how to tell the people that I love that they need help.

A friend of mine was having a bad time and was blaming it all on her boyfriend. From the outside looking in, I could see that it wasn't *all* his fault and I struggled to find the right words.

#138

May 18, 2010

No good deed goes unpunished.

Well, I found the words but apparently they were not the "right" words at all. We're not friends anymore.

#139

May 19, 2010

Everything's better with butter. (thanks, Paula!)

I do love me some Food Network!

#140

May 20, 2010

Don't ask the question if you're not prepared to hear the answer.

I'm fairly well-known for my cakes and cupcakes. I have a knack for it, particularly the icing. Many people tell me how much they like it and often ask for the recipe. It's not like it's some big secret like Colonel Sanders' Eleven Herbs and Spices but I always respond with, "If you like it and you want to continue to enjoy it, don't ask me that question." The silly fools who fail to heed my advice and insist I tell them anyway are more often than not brought to tears when they find out what is in my buttercream frosting. I'm just sayin', don't ask if you're not prepared to hear the answer.

May 21, 2010

#141

Life is neither fair nor equipped with an instruction booklet. Dammit. (and batteries are not included, double dammit)

The instruction booklet applies to all of us; the battery lament is especially important for us single girls in our thirties.

May 22, 2010

#142

Put your heart into everything you do; writing a thank you note, working hard at your job or school or even making a burger for good friends. Do it with love and sincerity and it will come back to you ten-fold.

There is a group of kids that I am particularly fond of; well, they're not kids anymore. They graduated from high school in 2004. I had many of them as juniors for history and then again as seniors for economics. There was just something about this group of friends that I enjoyed and we've remained close. On this night, I had them all over to my new house for dinner and then we went out downtown for a few drinks. They're all in their early 20s now and they call me "Mia" most of the time but they're still good friends with one another and I still adore them. God knew what He was doing when He put them in my life. ❤

#143

Clarity can come from the most shocking places. Just watched my Gramma flirt with the sexy male nurse at the hospital; I get it honest!

I couldn't make this up if I tried! My sister said it best, "He was hot!" It's true, he was. Still is, in fact. When a friend of mine was in the hospital in early December of the same year guess who the nurse was? Oh yeah! Let me just tell you, I visited with my friend just a bit longer and wore shoes just a bit sexier than maybe I normally would have.

#144

No matter how out of control of my life I feel at least I can take solace in the fact that I'm not Lindsay Lohan.

As the date of my surgery was looming over me, scheduled for the very next day, dear Ms. Lohan made the news again and I was suddenly feeling much better about myself. ☺ I must be a little bit psychic, too, because I'm all better and she's still a hot mess.

#145

There is something about a freshly-made bed that makes everything feel okay.

So, the morning of my surgery I had to be at the hospital very, very early. I got up early so I could wax extra well and because I just couldn't sleep. I made my bed and stared at it for a minute. I was thinking that it will feel really nice to come home and crawl into my lovely, freshly-made bed and that maybe it'll be a little easier to heal and wait patiently for the results of the tests they would be running. I was right. ☺

#146

Nothing is ever so broken that good friends and fabulous family can't fix.

I was in pain. I was in serious, major, even-hurts-to-cry pain. The hospital meds had worn off and the take-home meds might as well have been skittles. Seriously, I felt as though I had just been the star of a Tijuana Donkey Show. Since the doctor was unsure of exactly what was inside my tumor, he didn't want to remove it with a laparoscopic procedure. I was okay with that. I was not so okay with having him cut into my gullet and through the muscle but the thought of breaking that bad boy open inside of me and having it spill really did not sit well, either. And then, he told me that he wouldn't have to cut me at all. See, I come standard with a convenient opening perfect for just such an occasion. Oh.My.God.

That's right, my friends. I'm pretty sure he put on one of those helmets with the light on it and crawled right up there with all his equipment and a few buddies. I woke up with the worst case of sex hip *ever*. Girls, you know what I mean. Some of the fellas, too. So a few friends and family members took turns babysitting and bringing me food on trays. I made the command decision that the homemade white sangria I had made the previous weekend was part of my pain-management plan and I was a better woman for it. It hurt to laugh, so they cried with me when Crystal was robbed, robbed I say! on *American Idol* and poor, dear, sweet John knew not what to do when I sneezed and crumpled in pain, literally rendered speechless. In all, they took very, very good care of me and helped distract me from the torture that is waiting, waiting, waiting for the phone to ring to find out what that damn tumor was all about.

#147

May 27, 2010

Take pleasure in the details.

I tried to go back to work. I think I lasted an hour. There was no way I could sit up in an office chair. I *could* however sit back on my tail bone in a movie theatre so that is precisely what Beth and I did! We went to see *Sex and the City Two* and I kind of liked it so don't hate. (I was still self-medicating with Sangria and Xanax but whatever.) It was on the ride home, while in the drive-thru line at Starbucks, that the phone finally rang. The nurse in my doctor's office had two bits of news to share. My five-pound tumor was officially benign. Inside there were pre-cancer cells and ripe cancer-growing conditions but they were all completely contained and we had gotten it out before it bloomed. There was no evidence of any other cancerous cells anywhere else in the entire explored region. Now that's the kind of detail I like to hear.

Oh, no, that wasn't a typo. I really did write FIVE-POUND tumor. However, no sex for a few weeks and an internal ultra-sound every three months for the next couple of years was the plan of attack. My re-furbished uterus is ready for an occupant, if you know of anybody looking. just sayin'

#148

**Celebrate all victories- big and small-
and whenever possible do so with
Five Guys Burgers & Fries!**

I managed to go back to work today! I stayed the whole
day except for lunch when I went out with a few of the girls to
celebrate my triumphant return to being able to sit up.

#149

**Like a sprained ankle, I ain't nothin'
to play with!**

A few things to note well: Yes, I know it's from a rap song.
No, I don't know which one. Yes, I was *pissed* at someone I had
trusted and who had done me wrong. No, I'm not getting into it
here. Yes, I know that's annoying. No, I don't give a shit that you
bought this damn book and you want to know. Yes, I'm laughing
at you. No, I'm still not telling. Yes, it's all over now. No, the
person I trusted is no longer a part of my world.

#150

Possessions lead to insanity...

You think that you own a few things but really, they own
you.

#151 Technology is both a blessing and a curse.

Let's go ahead and add anger to the list of emotions that one should not be feeling when writing a text or sending an email or making a phone call.

20 years
Post-High School
Revelation

#152

Say what you mean, mean what you say; don't do it any other way. (little shout out to Mr. Gearhart for that gem! It applies even more today than it did in 8th grade.)

The only thing worse than a liar is someone who meely-mouths around and doesn't say what they mean. You know the people I'm talking about. They couldn't make a definitive statement if their life depended on it. I'm half-tempted to start actually threatening their lives if they can't give a straight answer. Ugh!

#153

Customer service has gone the way of the dinosaur.

Blackberry trackball + Verizon store = TOTAL FAIL

#154

Be sure to hit "dismiss" and not "snooze" on your extra-loud, extra-annoying cell phone alarm before jumping in the shower. The incessant ringing makes the normally refreshing showering experience rather stressful.

It's so bad that I sincerely debated jumping out of the shower with a head full of shampoo to turn it off. The only thing stopping me was the thought of having to go back to the Verizon store after I got the phone wet and it shit the bed agian.

June 4, 2010

#155

Hawkeye said it best on M*A*S*H when he noted that we're all entitled to Life, Liberty and the Pursuit of Happy Hour!

Oh, Friday; how I miss you all week long...

June 5, 2010

#156

The bitter taste of disappoint makes the flavor of opportunity and lessons well-learned that much sweeter.

Sue, "Damn I didn't want to think THAT hard on a HOT Saturday evening Mia!"

Mia, "Sorry, Suz! Happiness is a hard man, is that better? ☺"

Sue, "You betcha! Got any spares?????"

#157

Good friends will help you move but really good friends will help you move a body.

Lacy, "Which reminds me, we need to talk about that "thing." *wink wink*"

Zach, "oh go figure lacy murdered someone"

Taylor, "oooh is that why those boxes were so heavy?"

#158

You ARE your actions!

I don't separate a person from their behavior. You know what I mean, "Oh, she's really nice she just gets a little bitchy sometimes." No, she's just a bitch. "He's a heck of a good man, you can count on him for anything, he just cheats on his wife a lot." No, he's a pig. You don't like to be known as the behavior you display? Then change your behavior!

#159

It was exactly 20 years ago today that my RLHS classmates and I donned our caps & gowns and crowded into the oven that was the Red Land gym on a hot, humid, rainy night. We thought we were finally done. The truth is that we are just NOW hitting our stride! The best is yet to come...

By now, I had developed quite a little following on my facebook page. People were looking forward to my daily revelations, or perhaps deleting me because of them, it could go either way. My classmates from back in the day, however, had a few thoughts when I posted this one.

Larry, "I couldn't remember the date but I thought it was close I can't believe I'm still alive."

Theresa, "so hard to believe! I wonder what I'm going to be when I grow up?"

Jen, "Wow! Twenty years already!! Thanks for the reminder, Mia. It made my day!!"

Michael, "I remember being halfway to the stadium when they announced the change on Wink 104 because the storm was coming...what a fun, crazy night, I remember parts like it was yesterday. Sitting next to Steve near the back because we were so tall! ahhhh the memories!"

Larry, "I was almost there and ran into jeremy and turned around"

Mia, "I was at work, attempting to sell the devil my soul, so we could have the ceremony outside! He wasn't buying, the filthy bastard, but Jenna gave me an extra ticket so my Gramma could be in the gym so it was all good. ☺ It's so hard to believe that was 20 years ago!!"

Jen, "I think Belinda and I were driving up Reeser's Summit when we heard. Did we have rehearsal that day? Can't remember."

Heather, "We had rehearsal for the chorus at the outdoor stadium at Cedar Cliff and the rain started then... and we all trucked back to Red Land for graduation. Are you really sure that was 20 years ago? Um... I am not buying it! Deeeee----nile!"

June 9, 2010

#160

Today's revelation is courtesy of my 3-year old nephew. Girls don't have pee-pees. Boys have pee-pees. Girls have butts and butts. By all means, enjoy!

This is one of those times in my life when I wish I was the star of a reality TV show and there was a camera crew following me around and capturing everything. I was giving Abby and Ben a bath when Ben dropped that little gem on me. I really don't think there's anything I can say to add value to it.

June 10, 2010

#161

The opinions of people for whom you have no respect mean absolutely nothing.

Have you ever noticed how wound up people get about what other people think of them? It's a dirty, nasty habit and I'm proud that I've totally outgrown it. (Thank you, thirty-eight years of living and learning.) When all is said and done, it is the opinion of the people I respect the most that really matters to me. If you don't have my respect well, then, you might want to hang on to your opinion.

June 11, 2010

#162

All I really need are clear blue skies, a full tank of gas and a beach house for the weekend with the girls. OCMD, here I come!

Heather, Ang, Barb, Tawnia and Patty- THANK YOU for being in my world!

June 12, 2010

#163

Fat Bottomed Girls make the rockin' world go 'round!

Hell YES we do! ☺ (still at the beach, there may have been some dancing...)

June 13, 2010

#164

It's all a big numbers game, really. If you pass out often enough, you're bound to wake up with a Sharpie marker mustache or being dry-humped into submission a time or two.

At the time this book went to print, the judge had not yet ruled on the motion giving me permission to discuss this further. I will state, for the record, *I* do not have now, nor have I ever had, a mustache- Sharpie or otherwise.

June 14, 2010

#165

The waiting, indeed, is the hardest part!

Have we discussed my lack of patience? Yeah, I still don't have any…

June 15, 2010

#166

Life moves pretty fast; if you don't stop and look around once in a while you could miss it. (Thanks, Ferris!)

I really don't think that there is any hiccough in life that can't be addressed by an 80s classic; especially if John Hughes is running the show. I wrote the following blog back in March 2009 and re-posted it on facebook in August of that same year when John Hughes passed away. While the title may seem off-putting, it's really a tribute to the man who so definitively shaped my world-perception. You'll be missed, John Hughes!

Fuck You, John Hughes

Imagine my astonishment when I discovered that my life is not *Pretty in Pink*. I've blown out *Sixteen Candles* and felt *Some Kind of Wonderful* from time to time but *The Breakfast Club* of which I am a member never gets to take the day off with *Ferris Bueller*. I've ventured out into *The Great Outdoors*, been around the world in *Planes, Trains & Automobiles,* dabbled in some *Weird Science* and had *Career Opportunities* aplenty. However, I've been thinking about my 20-year high school *Class Reunion* next year and the more I think about it I really just want to stay *Home Alone*. Sadly, hiding from that which is scary is for *Only the Lonely* and if I want even a chance at starring in my own version of *She's Having a Baby* I need to surrender the fantasy and embark an *American Adventure* on my own terms.

I don't really hate or blame John Hughes. The title of this blog is just clever. And it rhymes. He had a fantasy world for sale and oh baby, I was buying! I thought for sure that at the end of the catchy, 80's-music-backdropped-montage I would be kissing the handsome star. I did get to kiss him once or twice but the dirty little trick that John Hughes didn't tell me was that after the screen fades to black, after the closing credits and the studio logo leave the screen, it's up to me to write the next chapter of the story.

You know, I don't even mind being the author. I'll write the next chapter, even a few sequels- no problem. The problem arises then the other characters in my story don't want to play anymore. There has been a time or two when I wanted to go star in another show and once a character was killed off. Real life is not a daytime soap so he's not coming back from the dead. That's been a bitter pill to swallow. It's made my character stronger, more interesting, I think. It's the characters, and sometimes the circumstances, that prefer to improvise rather than follow my script that are my challenge. It really would all go so much smoother if everyone just did what I said.

There would be drama, I'm sure, as I am certainly a purveyor of drama. There would be comedy, too. I need to laugh out loud at least nine times a day to feel complete. And the sex scenes, hot damn! They will be steamy. I am quite the connoisseur. At first glance it would be simply perfect. Serendipitous, if you will. However, there's a catch.

I love people who disagree with me. I like to think about things from a different angle. Anyone who forces me to think outside the box is a keeper in my world. Ergo, I fill my show with free-thinkers, those with free-will and more often than not that will is equal to my own. Dammit. And so, I must learn the lesson John Hughes never intended: patience. All the world is a stage and we fools are mere players and I'll be damned if I'm not starring in the show. So, I study patience; I am learning my lesson slowly and well because, after all, the show must go on...

June 16, 2010

#167 The very best gifts- whether to give or to receive- are the ones on which more time than money has been spent.

There is a tendency to try to show your love and affection in the classic American-fashion: bigger, better, faster, more! But truthfully, all the things I've appreciated most have not been expensive gifts. It's the thoughtful time spent in choosing the perfect gift. Often times, it's something handmade and really quite cheap.

#168

Early summer arrives bringing humidity and mating season; and the entire world loses its freakin' mind.

I have curly hair and I'm happiest when I can see my breath. Summer and me? Not so much…

#169

I am still in awe of the capacity of my friends and family to be loving, generous and compassionate. Thank you all for being in my life!

Some of my revelations are not necessarily focused on the day or something happening in my life at that moment. Many are just generalizations of things I've learned at some point along the way.

#170

A house is not a home until there is a blender of margaritas whirring on the counter. ☺

And then there are revelations like this one; I was simply excited about my new blender.

#171

No matter how many kisses you get, some boo-boos just never heal. I miss you, Daddy; Happy Father's Day. ♥

I miss my dad. I miss him like a fat kid at camp misses cake. He was my hero, my biggest cheerleader and my #1 fan. He was way too young to die in a stupid accident that could have easily been prevented. I think that's what makes the missing of him all that much worse. He didn't have to die at the age of forty-six. He just didn't. He should be alive and well right now enjoying his grandchildren, scolding my bad choices and celebrating my success. Instead, I sit here seventeen years later and I miss him. Wear your seat belt; don't drink and drive. Please. Do that for me and maybe he didn't die in vain.

#172

I much prefer the idea of the first day of summer to the reality. The concept of the changing of the season, the circle of life, etc. is far better than the bleeping heat that won't quit for at least three months. *sigh*

Good Lord, Gladys; I hate the heat. I hate it! I hate it as much as the sun-worshipers hate the cold. Here's my theory, though: you can always put on another pair of socks or a sweater, you can't take off your skin.

#173
I am thoroughly content with what I have but never with what I am. The day I think I have nothing more to learn will be the day I begin to die.

I spent a great deal of time when I was younger acquiring stuff. I remember, as a young, dumb wife, standing in my living room looking around at all my stuff and thinking, "This is all mine!" (I already admitted that I was young and dumb; don't give me any shit for not recognizing that I was missing the whole concept of sharing as an integral part of marriage.) I've gone through a few phases and evolutions in my life and completely transfused all of my stuff a few times. The stuff doesn't really matter. It can disappear twice as quickly as it can be acquired, but who I am, the thoughts and knowledge that I acquire, can never be lost or replaced. In the long run, the stuff doesn't mean shit.

#174
I'm not in charge; that's the only way I know for sure that I'm not in hell.

Ugh, my job. At this point in the summer, I didn't know what would come to pass over the next three months. It was a horrendous task to learn the job but even after I'd gotten a handle on it the time spent at my office was relentless. I don't mind working hard, but my home-work balance was way off center. All I knew for sure was that I was seriously beginning to hate it and relating more and more every single day to Melvin in *Office Space*.

#175

If he's stupid enough to walk away then be smart enough to let him.

I am fairly certain credit for this little gem must go to my fabulous friend, Lacy. It's a fantastic sentiment and I'm totally on board with the theory, but the practice of it I really struggle with. I think I became a teacher because somewhere inside of me I believe everyone is capable of learning, (read: changing), and that I have the inherent talent to facilitate that comprehension, (read: change.) I don't teach teenagers anymore but I think I still try to "teach" the men in my life how to treat me. What I really need to be doing is turning that fantastic talent I have for teaching on myself and learn how to let go when it's just not right. Fuck. That's really hard to do. just sayin'

#176

June 25, 2010

Chinese food via delivery makes me feel like all is right with the world.

At the job from hell there were a few bright spots. My girl, Meesh, was one of them. We ordered Chinese food and snarfed it down in my office. It.Was.Awesome.

#177

June 26, 2010

Life isn't about waiting for the storm to pass. It's about learning to dance in the rain.

Todra, "This is one of the coolest ones yet! love it."

Tabitha, "That is the best saying ever! I really do try to live that way....every once in awhile it's nice to be reminded. ☺"

Mia, "T&T, I'm not much into pity or playing the poor, poor me game but I liked this one especially today. Three years ago today my mom lost her fight with ALS but now I work for the hospice that took care of her. My little dance in that rain storm."

Michael, "You go ahead and DANCE girl!"

June 27, 2010

#178   The sweetest victory, hands down, is the defeat of your own, personal demons.

My mom and I spent our entire life on earth together trying to understand one another, failing to do so, and wondering why, good God why, the other was so...<insert your own adjective here.> Unfortunately, my mom died before she could defeat her own demons here on earth. I have great faith that on the other side, she's found peace. As for me, as much as I wish she and I could have come to a greater understanding in the living years and had the *Gilmore Girls* relationship I always wanted, I had to surrender because it was never, ever going to happen. Letting go of the impossible has made all other things possible.

#179

I sincerely regret having refused those naps as a child.

Mondays at work after having been up late on Sunday are brutal. I'm sure you understand.

#180

Speak your mind even if your voice shakes.

I saw this bumper sticker when I was walking in the morning before work. Then, I got to the job that I was already starting to hate, and there was a shit storm in the works looking for a scapegoat. Now, I'm no scapegoat. If I'm wrong I can own it and do my best to fix it but this leads me directly to the next revelation...

#181

I'm not your bitch; don't put your shit on me.

Another early-morning walk revelation, courtesy of the Madonna song that came on the iPod. I'm nobody's bitch and I have enough shit of my own; I don't need any of yours.

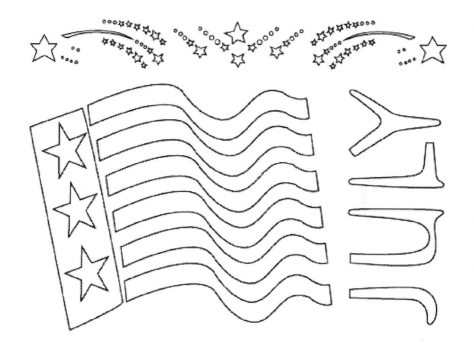

20 years
Post-High School
Revelation

#182

If the sun has risen and set and you have not doubled over in laughter you have wasted a chance you'll never have again.

Don't over think it; just find something hysterical every day.

#183

I freakin' hate shopping.

I probably wouldn't hate it as much if I had unlimited funds and a size six body.

#184

Table #10 is the coolest table at the wedding!

Jeff and Katie got married. Congratulations! Also, thank you for placing Beth and me at the same table with Mike, Dee, Megan, Joey, Marc, Brook, Adam and Nici. A good time was most definitely had by all. ☺

#185

All men are created equal and endowed by their creator with certain inalienable rights; among these are life, liberty and the pursuit of happiness. Happy 234th America! God Bless you and those who wear your flag on their shoulders to always keep this the land of the free and the home of the brave!!

#186

I like Pina Coladas, getting caught in the rain...

John, "NOTICE: Johnny and Mia will be making love at midnight, in the dunes of the cape. You may now go back to your regularly scheduled facebooking."

Patty, "I hate that song."

#187

I am strong; I am invincible, except when it comes to a migraine in a heat wave...

Okay, so we've already covered how much I hate the heat and let me tell you, the summer of 2010 was freakin' brutal. Add to that the fact that my a/c sucks electricity like a crack whore jonesing for a fix and you've got yourself a recipe for disaster. Throw a migraine on top of it and I was one miserable bitch. God bless you, the makers of prescription-strength pain killers...

July 7, 2010

#188
Three things that cannot be long hidden; the sun, the moon and the truth. (shout out to Buddha for teaching me this one)

Another bumper sticker; this time in the parking lot at Staples. It struck me how perfect and divine the universe is that I saw this on a day when I was struggling to come up with a clever revelation and I was having some trouble with a nasty little under-the-bus-thrower at work. Oh.My.God, I was hating that job! I had to desperately hang on to the idea that as the sun and moon rise to the top in their own time, so will the truth. This little find really helped me find the extra ounce of strength that I needed.

July 8, 2010

#189
Just when I get myself good and jaded, the Universe shows me hope and possibility; Happy Anniversary Micah & Lacy!

My friends, Micah and Lacy, were married on 07-08-09. They both know all too well the bitter taste of heartache and disappointment and managed to find one another in the abyss. They fell in love, got married, had a baby and forced me to see that maybe, just maybe, it's not too late for me.

#190

Power only has value in its ability to do good things. Do Good. Be Powerful. Paint with Purpose.

I was still raising money for the Susan G. Komen 3-day walk for Breast Cancer and organized this evening at a local ceramics studio. A portion of all the proceeds would be donated to my overall goal. Naturally, I shamelessly promoted it on facebook.

#191

People plan; God laughs.

#192

Beauty lies in simplicity.

Is there anything better than a quiet Sunday, all to yourself, to do your chores and lounge around with your kitties? I'll go ahead and answer that for you. No! No, there most certainly is not. The beautiful simplicity of nothingness is a luxury I am so very rarely afforded so when it comes along I try to hold on to it tight. With both hands. Not the kitties, though, they tend to holler when you hold them too tight. They're finicky that way.

#193

Stand your ground, use your words, tell the truth and archive every e-mail

Oh, the shit hit the fan! There's this one horrible, horrible bitch at work who decided that the best way to make it okay that she fucked up was to make it someone else's fault. She tried to make that someone me. Ha ha ha, joke's on you, you quack! I have a spine, I am not afraid to speak up and I keep ALL correspondence! Now, don't worry, we're quickly coming to the point where I escape the job I had wanted so badly but now I absolutely hate, but for now- at this point in our story- I'm still stuck there. Damn bills.

#194

Always fly high and proud; not low and into the windshield like that pretty, little, yellow finch this morning on my way to work. May he rest in peace.

Okay, so here's the worst part of this little vignette. Not only did this actually happen on the way to work that morning, but the tiny little corpse got stuck on my windshield and rode all the way to the office with me! I couldn't stop crying and begging God to please, please, please let it not have felt any pain. Then I took a picture of it with my phone and posted it on facebook with the revelation. I didn't say I was right in the head.

#195

It's good to have the rug pulled out from underneath you from time to time. It gives you a chance to notice if you were standing on terra firma or on a pile of bullshit.

I had this friend. We were friends for a long, long time. Then I found out that she was absolutely, freakin' nuts and some of it started to spill over and get on me. I told her to keep her crazy to herself and then we weren't friends anymore. I miss my friend, but the crazy is just too overwhelming so there you have it. On this day, however, she had just tried to pull a fast one on me. (We were in the process of breaking up the friendship at this point and it was getting a little messy.) It's okay, though. I'm glad she tried to really screw me over. It helped remind me what I was made of and I knew I was going to need that strength to go back to work and deal with the back-stabbing bitch. At least only until the damn Powerball finally goes my way.

#196

After all is said and done, anything I've ever accomplished that was worth the effort was something that, at first, scared the shit out of me.

Scott, "so, you are saying potty training scared you....literally?"

Jenn, "I hope you are collecting all of these for your next book. It would be a good one to have for reference. ☺"

Mia, "Scotty, I don't remember potty training- I was done by age 2!! Jen, I am indeed! ☺"

Scott, "everything comes back to number 2"

July 16, 2010

#197

Don't lament coming late to the party but rather celebrate daring to show up at all.

It's never too late to jump on the right bandwagon.

July 17, 2010

#198

There's no such thing a pleasant, character building, afternoon. Good character comes from living through the worst and learning something about yourself in the process.

Nothing good comes easy.

July 18, 2010

#199

If you take an extra helping of Saturday night then Sunday morning will demand full restitution.

I think this one is rather self-explanatory, but I'll expand ever-so-slightly. The night before I went out with a few friends to celebrate Gina's twenty-first birthday. In the process, I seemed to have forgotten that I was waayyyy beyond twenty-one and certainly should not be drinking like a twenty-one-year-old. And so, this Sunday morning, ahem, early afternoon, revelation was born. As the fabulous **Bethie** put it, "Haaaaaaaaa haaaaaaaaaaaaa haaaaaaaaaaaa! That's the nicest way of saying, 'I've got one hell of a hangover'...I have EVER heard!"

#200

(with a little help from Margaret Mead) Never doubt that a small group of thoughtful, committed citizens can change the world. Indeed, it is the only thing that ever has. Be thoughtful and committed with me tonight at Color Me Mine!

A milestone. My 200th revelation and the night of my fundraiser for the Susan G. Komen foundation. Indeed, a good time was had by all and money was raised for one hell of a good cause!

#201

The Dollar Tree is shady. Just so you know, if you over-buy items for a fundraiser and try to return the un-opened extras with your receipt after having paid cash, they will not refund your money or issue store credit. You must make an exchange right then and there. Bastards...

Of course, the next day I tried to increase our funding by returning the items, un-opened and with the receipt, that I did not need and I was *denied* by the evil bitches at The Dollar Tree.

#202

Sometimes you have to surrender your own agenda for that of the people you love; my sister is looking for nice, wooden frame bunk beds for my nephew and my brother is looking for someone who wants the tree that fell in his back yard for firewood. Firewood is free, bunk beds on the cheap, please. ☺

You'll be pleased to know that my brother's yard is fallen-tree-free and my nephew is sleeping on the bottom bunk of a beautiful set of wooden bunk beds. He is hoping to be allowed to sleep on the top bunk one of these days but the rule my sister has set forth is that he needs to have ten green light days in a row. For those of you unfamiliar with the stoplight system, allow me to enlighten you. ha ha ha You evaluate the child's behavior on a traffic light. A green light is really good behavior; following the rules, minding manners, etc. If he or she starts to act up then a warning is in order and you move the child's marker to yellow. If the behavior either continues to worsen or does not improve, then the marker goes onto the red light. My darling nephew is an Aquarius and full of energy, ergo, he does not spend a lot of time on the green light.

My sister, his mother, really doesn't want to let him sleep on the top bunk. I can't say I blame her as it is a long way down to the floor below and she *did* make him from scratch. She isn't thrilled with the idea of him getting broken: he's small, the floor is hard. This is why she decreed that he may not sleep on the top bunk until he has ten green light days in a row.

Let the record show that I am writing this in late December 2010 and that, to my knowledge, Ben has not yet slept on the top bunk.

#203

The sexier the shoe the more the pain; but I don't give a damn! I wear them anyway.

Ladies, why do we do this to ourselves?

#204

It might mean a lot of Smack Ramen and Weis brand diet cola but the thought of time to write, sleep in and lounge around at the river makes unemployment compensation look mighty attractive! (bring it on, Ody!)

The day I wrote this I was hating my job even more than usual and there was no end in sight. I was seriously dreaming about getting laid off so I could just write and lounge all summer long but I really needed that payday so I couldn't just quit. Unemployment, oh my, the thought of that was even sexier than some of the shoes I own. Some.

#205

Alcohol preserves everything except dignity.

Ahhh, Second Street on a Saturday night. We meet again…

#206

Today is as good as any to go back to square one and do it right this time.

Ahhh, Sunday morning after a Saturday night on Second Street. We clean up last night's mess again...

#207

The only things you regret in this life are the chances you didn't take. Ann-Margaret said this in *Grumpy Old Men* and it is so fabulously true!

I absolutely love this quote. I'm a go for it kind of girl; just do it. I was still looking for a way out of the job I hated. Hadn't quite found it yet, but I was willing to take the chance the instant it presented itself.

#208

If you feel the urge to state the obvious then by all means resist it. You will NOT curry favor with the person assaulted with your redundant "observation."

You need to know before I continue to bitch about the job I hate that I was freakin' brilliant at it. No, not at first. At first I was a bumbling idiot but once I got the hang of it I was a bona fide rock star. I was in charge of admissions at a hospice care agency. I coordinated the clinical, financial and legal information for all potential patients and arranged the personnel to verify it. If there was a doctor that needed to be contacted or an insurance company to be tangled with- I was the go-to gal. I hated my job because it was so, so far away from the ideal it should have been and I worked with a couple of seriously evil people who were so not human. I went to work there because they had taken care of my mom when she was sick and dying and they were fantastic! I wanted to give back. Well, in the three years since my mom died they had become a colony of evil, money-grubbing pricks who don't seem to give two shits about the patients they care for or about the people who do the caring.

On this particular day, one of those evil pricks had popped a head in my office and asked if I had verified the insurance yet on patient X, because without the insurance we couldn't take care of the patient. Really? Really?! Is that how this whole thing works? I wanted to hurl the office supplies and flower vase within reach at that head with all the strength I have- and that day being a menstrual day we're talking *a lot* of strength- but instead I took my anger and frustration to facebook where my friends made me laugh. And saved the life of that prick.

Michael, "Wait a second...didn't you just do that 208 times! Love ya Mia!"

Craig, "Please forward all future "redundant observations" to the Department of Redundancy Department."

Mia, "ha ha ha, funny, Mike! We thank you for your input, Craig, and we thank you."

PS yes, I had already verified the insurance... *sigh*

#209

Andy Gibb was my first love and I still miss him; after all, love is thicker than water. *sigh*

All of my Barbies made out with and were married to Andy Gibb. Sure, he looked like Ken but that was just the disguise that he wore so he wouldn't get hounded by the paparazzi.

#210

You'll meet most people by chance, by choice you may become friends but if God is charitable enough to let you fall in love don't let anything get in the way of enjoying every blessed second.

#211

Sometimes you just have to say, "What the fuck?"

To be perfectly honest, I don't know why I was just saying "what the fuck" on this day, but some friends of mine made me laugh so hard I didn't even care anymore.

Cristina, "OMG Mia! No one actually says it anymore, they say WTF....LOL"

Craig, ""She's just an old fashion girl, a traditionalist if you will. She learned to use foul language the old school way, like a lady should. There's no substituting her words for letters, oh no not this girl. Say it loud, say it proud. 'I swear like a drunken sailor, so fuck you and the horse you rode in on'"

July 31, 2010

#212

When the Xanax must be rationed it's time to panic.

The story I'm about to tell you is 100% true. Brace yourself.

Have you ever been to a family reunion? No, not your brothers and sisters, a rogue grandparent and a random cousin. I'm talking about a big one where it's all the extended family you never knew you had and even though you're all related you need name tags. We're talking hundreds of people.

Side Note: Schroeder is Filipino; he went to one of his family reunions once and found himself making out with some chick he met there before realizing she was a cousin. He explained later that *that* was the day he starting dating white girls because he knew he wasn't related to any of them. Yeah, he wasn't too bright and I got over the novelty of dipping my toe into that particular little interracial dating pool.

Anyway, so I'm at this family reunion which really isn't so bad. Honestly. The food is decent and there's a lot of family I enjoy and hadn't seen in a long, long time. Plus, it really made my Gramma happy to have us all there together so despite it feeling like I was in an episode of *The Cake Boss* it was not an unpleasant experience. In hindsight, I'm really glad I went because my Aunt Mary was there. She was 95 and my Gramma's last sister. She passed away four months later, so I was really truly happy to have been able to spend some time with her that day.

But then, the text came. Please note that the date of this revelation. The next day would be August 1. August 1 being the day the first year law student was to pay his security deposit and first month's rent for two bedrooms and a bathroom share in my house. I had turned others down because lawyer boy seemed like a good fit and had the financial backing of his grandmother. I emphasize seemed because the text that arrived one day before his money was due informed me that he had found another place to live and thanks, but no thanks. Son.of.a.bitch!!

As if the text were not enough, my sister said to me moments later, "You ready? We need to get going." Now, rest assured; I love my sister and her kids and I think her boyfriend is a real stand-up guy. It was fantastic to pile into the 'ol minivan with Meg, Joey and the kids for a fun little road trip there; very little traffic, a DVD player to entertain the kids and a nap. I was not at all unhappy. However, we had to get the kids back home because they had plans with their dad so the trip home was on a time schedule that we couldn't control.

Traffic.

A lot of it.

And I had only three Xanax left in the bottle.

Time to panic.

Meg sold the minivan not long after that. Some bad ju ju just can't be prayed away...

AUGUST

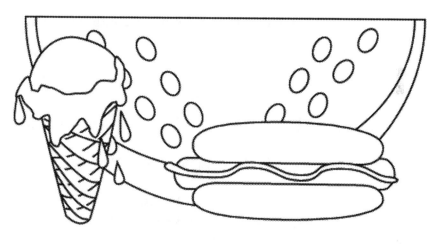

20 years
Post-High School
Revelation

#213

When someone screws you over, don't bother to sue them; the courts are way too slow. I like to curse their bowels instead. I'll never get the money back anyway, but it's comforting to know I've made them suffer in the worst way possible.

Lawyer Boy, you little fucker; I hope you didn't shit right for a month.

#214

Wear your seat belt. Period.

I lost a former student the day before due to the lack of a seat belt. Please, spend the seconds it takes to click it into place. Please.

#215

Don't assume giving up is weakness; be strong enough to let go.

I paraphrased this one from my friend, Holly, who was going through a tough time of her own. I thought considering the line of work I was in, how much I was hating my job, (hating the company, really- still loved working in hospice care), witnessing the pain of the aftermath of another soul gone too soon and just being introspective in general that it was speaking directly to me. Thanks, Holly. ☺

#216

A little faith can take your soul to heaven but great faith will bring heaven to your soul.

Those who have no faith and those who lack the courage to attempt faith will never know the peace it brings to the heart.

#217

What I'm really looking for is a sugar daddy, a schmuck; someone to pay bills & do as told, who I can control & walk all over, probably cheat on, but who'll still indulge my every whim & tolerate my bad behavior. I want to get married NOW, have a baby before my bio clock explodes & my eggs expire & then I want to kick him out of the million-dollar home he buys for me so I can shack up w/ the pool boy.

There was a slightly longer, funnier version of this one but facebook stifles creativity with a character limit. Even so, my cousin, **Rob**, the king of all rants, declared it awesome and my sister, **Megan**, said it was sheer genius but it was a friend of mine who really brought the funny.

Mia, "If my status made you snicker and/or smile, by all means enjoy my Thursday funnies. If it made you recoil and stammer or in some manner fear me then clearly you've got issues too big for me to handle; not the least of which is the inability to recognize and appreciate sarcasm."

Craig, "Maybe you can use the pool boy we had when the kids were younger. I don't know why we needed one, all we had was one of those little hard plastic K-Mart pools, but Anna insisted. Wait a minute.........ANNA."

Anna is a friend of mine, too. She's married to Craig and gets to laugh at his antics a lot more often than the rest of us. Lucky Anna. Craig is currently serving overseas and I send him my gratitude, love and prayers for a safe return home. Please take a moment to offer a prayer of your own for my dear friend and for all who serve.

August 6, 2010

#218
There are really only three ingredients in a recipe for happiness: something to do, something to hope for and something to love.

August 7, 2010

#219
I still love, think of and miss you every single day; Happy Birthday, Daddy. ♥

My dad would have been 63.

#220

is too long for a status, it's in my note titled "Dating circa 2010." By all means, enjoy...

Dating circa 2010

Hi, I have a little favor to ask. Take a moment to do a bit of introspection and ask yourself, am I one of these men?

MR. MAYBE

He says he wants a woman who says what she means but then runs and hides when she does. For example:

HIM: Maybe we can get together tomorrow night.

HER: Maybe doesn't really work for me, if tomorrow's no good for you another time, then.

HIM: I have to see about work, I'll text you if I can make it.

HER: No, thank you, let me know when you can make plans with me and we'll get together.

HIM: Why are you rushing me?!

ONLY-WANTS-TO-GET-LAID

He's quick to reply to emails & texts, appears to be legitimate, fun & flirty but as soon as meeting for a drink in a public bar is suggested he counter-offers with come over to his place to cuddle & watch a movie. Then asks if you shaved down under.

Are you kidding me? If I wanted a random hook up I would go out at 1:45 AM and pick up a drunken douche bag. When I hold fast to my meet-in-public-no-sex-is-promised rule, suddenly he hems and haws about how he has to work. Okay, then, have a good one...

WAITING FOR MY EX TO COME HOME

If your ex is in every story you tell and every joke you make- even at her expense, if you're sure to point out, multiple times, how much you can't stand her and are glad she's gone, I'm thinking you've got a few things to work out. Good luck with that, sincerely, it's not easy.

MR. MONEYBAGS

If you're feeling compelled to tell me how much money you make, how much your mortgage is, all about the cars, boats, motorcycles, etc. that you own, that I can order anything I like since money is no object then I am going to assume that your penis is only two-inches long and doesn't always work. Is that really the message you want to send?

THE SALES REP

We all have two ears and one mouth so we should listen twice as much as we speak. If you spend all your time telling me all about how fabulous you are and make no effort to get to know me then I'm going with another proposal. I'd like to form my own opinion about you, thanks; not take the guided tour.

ÜBER-NERVOUS

If you feel there is a chance you will spend the entire evening staring at me with a goofy smile on your face and taking deep breaths to calm your nerves then maybe you're not quite ready to be dating. It's really quite exhausting to have to carry the entire conversation and way creepy to be stared at the whole night. Oh, and just in case you ignore my advice and ask me out anyway, don't go for the kiss. It's not going to end well for you.

PEN PAL

You don't really want a 3-D relationship; you just want to email, facebook, text and maybe once in a while chat on the phone. Well, good for you but I want to have sex so buh-bye!

#1 DAD!

You love your kids. You love spending time with your kids. You love talking about your kids and how much you love them and love spending time with them. Good for you and good for your kids! That's the way it should be. Here's a news flash: I'm not your kid nor do I want to be. I had a dad, he was awesome, not looking for another one. If you can't be both a dad and a man at the same time then just go be a dad.

Fellas, if you recognize yourself in any of those men then please, I beg you, delete my number, un-friend me, don't strike up a conversation or buy me a drink and sure as hell don't ask my friends to put in a good word for you! I have been to the puppet show and I have seen the strings.

I'm looking for what everyone is: effortless perfection. ☺ I'll settle for good conversation, great sex, a go-to plus one when I need it, someone to run away with for the weekend and to come home to. I'd love to have a baby or two, but that clock is seriously ticking and if I run out of time I need someone who won't resent me for it.

I'm not into games, drama or bullshit. I don't want to have to play hard-to-get or guess-what-he's-thinking. I don't know how to change a tire or hang blinds and I have no intention of learning but I will cook and do the laundry no problem.

Sometimes I like to snuggle, sometimes I don't want to be touched but I am always able to verbalize how I feel. I need to laugh everyday and I need to feel important & valued. There is no worse feeling than being ignored.

Okay, so there is it. The rant of the single girl in her 30's. Sadly, each and everything I've written is from personal experience.

Umm, yeah, this was written on a Sunday morning after a disastrous week that included a sudden, unexpected death, my father's birthday and three really bad first dates. Doesn't make it any less true, though, as evidenced by the comments it received.

Megan, "that... was... awesome..."

Mia, "Thanks, Megs. ☺"

Karolyn, "I'm sorry you've had to experience all of those 'boys' but you will find the right guy, just stay positive and he'll pop up where you least expect it. ☺ Love you!!"

Megan, "wow, very well said cuz ☺"

Kate, "Love it mia...I know how you feel lol...."

Mia, "Thanks, girls. I think I'll just hold out for Eric Northman; he can bite me anytime!"

Lacy, "Mia I wish you would be clearer about how you feel."

Jenn, "A-MEN sister!"

Donna, "I think you deserve the best, whoever that turns out to be. And since he'll be the best, he'll be worth the wait. I do understand how frustrating it can be; in the meantime."

Cassandra, "Will you write my dating website summary 'cause his is perfect ☺. I've only been single for 6 months and I can already relate soooo well to this. Good writing. ☺"

Cassandra, "Uh..his should be this. Kind of changes my meaning...lol"

Mia, "Thanks, Cass! I'll help anyway I can, but having been dating off & on for 25 years- both online and in the real world- I can say with authority that it's all equally fucked up. ☺"

Cassandra, "I recently met mr waiting for my ex and just want to get laid all in one...what a goober and waste of time lol"

Mia, "At least he was considerate enough to consolidate for you. ☺ Mr. Über-Nervous is 100% true, I simultaneously felt sorry for and was totally creeped out by him."

Sue, "This is also the rant of a 60-year-old woman! You did good Mia!"

Ah, yes, the dating world. Has there ever been a richer inspirational environment? I think not. The bit below was written before this project began, in fact I wrote it when I was dating Schroeder, the cousin-kissing Filipino, but I think it's absolutely appropriate to share here. And this is my freakin' book; I can write what I want! Learn it. Love it. Live it.

The Ten Commandments of Dating according to Mia

I. I am your date tonight. You shall have no other dates concurrent with me. If you should have to speak to another woman during the course of our date, do not allow that conversation to affect your mood and feeling toward me. I did not do whatever it is that she did, I am choosing to be here with you now.

II. Do not say my name wrong. If, for some reason, you can't remember how to pronounce it or have a momentary lapse of memory about just what it is, improvise, but do not call me by another's name. Ever.

III. Keep holy the day after. You have 24 hours to call, text, e-mail, smoke signal- something. If it was a bad date, man up and say goodbye. If it was a good date and you'd like another go at some point then don't let 24 hours pass without some form of communication. (If you can replace the word "date" with the word "sex" then this commandment counts as double.)

IV. Honor my mother and my father, the rest of my family, my friends, my pets, etc. by keeping your opinions to yourself until I ask for them. Compliments are the exception to this commandment, but only if they're sincere.

V. Thou shall not be a buzz kill. Ever.

VI. Thou shall not commit alternaty. Do not glance around the room, seeking alternatives, when you are with me. If you can't look at me when I'm all dressed up and putting on my best for you then why should I let you touch me later?

VII. Thou shall not steal my thunder. Before we go out, I will have removed hair, polished & painted assorted body parts, sold my soul to the hair-styling devil, carefully applied perfume, chosen jewelry & attire and I probably changed my mind 17 times before settling on just the look I wanted to show you. To not notice is essentially theft of my effort.

VIII. Thou shall not lie. Ever.

IX. Thou shall not want to be with my friends more than me. Or your friends. Or anyone else, for that matter. If that is how you feel, refer back to commandment #3, man up and say goodbye.

X. Thou shall not assume or put me in a position to be forced to make assumptions. If we can't communicate then we can't date.

#221

The only thing I hate more than Medicare is Medicaid.

You think your job sucks? Try tangling with these fuckers every day.

#222

Every tear I've shed has only made every smile that much sweeter.

I make a lot of jokes about dating and how much it sucks and looking for a good man but the truth of the matter is that I know what a broken heart feels like and I hate it. It's true that I appreciate joy and happiness better after having known a broken heart, but still. Ouch.

#223

Steven Slater is so totally a modern-day hero! He is Peter Gibbons brought to life. PS, if you don't know one or both of these names then you need to seriously reconsider our friendship.

Thank you, Jet Blue, for giving me a new verb to use at the office. For example, "If that bitch comes in here one more time I'm going to throw my stapler at her head and then Jet Blue my ass right out the window!"

#224

Even more than a good sense-of-humor, it's the appreciation of the ironic that has helped me avoid many a broken heart. It takes a good sense-of-irony to laugh at yourself.

Annddd...we're back to whining about men. I can do it, though. I can laugh at myself. I mean, I did make that horrible picture of me from the Bret Michaels' concert my profile pic!

#225

There is no harsher hurt than watching the people you love in pain. Please keep my best friend and her family in your loving thoughts and prayers. ♥

Had to get serious today. My best friend's mom had been sick off and on since we were just kids and this time when her cancer came back there was nothing more to do. Sadly, both my bff and I understand hospice and believe in it but when it's your own family it's not so easy.

#226

You can't take the victory lap if you don't enter the race. On that note, I just registered for the 2nd Annual Harrisburg Cupcake Cup! Any thoughts on what flavor I should enter?

Sadly, I didn't get to actually follow through and participate in the contest. You'll read more about my job and money woes in a bit but when I had to make the choice between bills and buying the supplies to enter the contest I chose bills. Fuckin' responsibility.

#227

Love almost always begins in laughter, explodes in passion and ends in heartache.

Megan, "Today's is depressing..."

Mia, "I know, Meg; but I tend to go with whatever my mood is for the day. I can't be Mary-freakin-sunshine all the time."

#228

I hate that I have so much practice with death, dying & grief. I miss the bliss of ignorance.

Still feeling a little blue and hurting for my best friend.

#229

Love is a strange business; the only way to make a profit is to give away your entire inventory for free.

Hey, look at that...a light at the end of the tunnel.

#230

I totally deserve a Powerball jackpot.

The entire world runs on a spreadsheet. It's true. There is a spreadsheet at the heart of every business and, for sure, every government entity. I have one, too. It has all the names of the people and causes I will be sharing with when I win the Powerball jackpot. I have it broken down by percentage so all I'll have to do is plug in the total amount I win and it calculates from there. My sister has seen it, she periodically inquires to be sure she is still on it. Her percentage fluctuates based on the quality of the birthday and Christmas gifts she gives me, but she's still there and so are her kids. My plans for vacations and plastic surgery are on there in VIP positions as are the charities I believe in. Here's a hot tip: Asking to be put on the spreadsheet is the fastest way to get banned from it. just sayin'

August 19, 2010

#231

As a matter of fact I DO mind if you ask for my zip code, phone number, email, and NO I do not want to apply for a credit card! I just want to pay cash for the one thing I need and go home!

I get a little cranky when I have to go shopping.

August 20, 2010

#232

Peanut Butter is, without a doubt, on the Top Ten List of "The Most Disgusting Things Humans Eat."

Look, I don't want to hear it. I hate peanut butter. I hate the look, the taste and the smell. When I have to cook with it for some torturous reason, I wear a mask. It is vile. It is disgusting. If you want to eat it go right ahead but I do not. I also hate ketchup and barbecue sauce. Don't try to change me; just be glad that there's more for you and move on.

August 21, 2010

#233

Life IS like a box of chocolates! Today my Gramma turned 84- Happy Birthday, Gram! Two of my favorite students got married, my five-year-old niece cheered in her very first scrimmage and my best friend laid her mother to rest. You never know what the day might bring.

August 22, 2010

#234

I don't know how it happened, but an hour has gotten shorter since I was a kid; for sure, 24 of them are not nearly enough in a day.

Don't come at me with your laws of physics, you know I speak the truth!

August 23, 2010

#235

How people treat you is their karma; how you react is yours. (thank you, Wayne Dyer)

The thing about karma is that, like justice, she's blind.

August 24, 2010

#236

Staff meetings are adult punishment for all the fun things I did as a teenager...

I'm telling you, I HATED that company! And my friend, Meesh, had given her notice so it was about to get even worse. Then I had to sit in a staff meeting. *sigh*

#237

When an irresistible woman meets a stubborn-as-hell, unmovable man the result is an endless transfer of energy, i.e. passion, baby. Pure passion.

If I actually confess who I had been talking to and detailed the conversation that led to the writing of this revelation you're going to think I'm totally pathetic. I will admit that it was one hell of a hot phone call...

#238

I might be indecisive, I'm not sure.

Pssst...can you keep a secret? I had an interview on this day for a new job! It went really, really well but it was a bit of a gamble. I had to decide if I was going to take it because he had already told me he was prepared to offer me the position. ☺

Side Note: My first meeting of Impatience Anonymous was that same night. I could *not* wait!

#239

Anything you say in a drunken stupor is forgiven if you're drinking with a chaplain.

It was the best of times. It was the worst of times. I was out with the people from work who I actually really, really liked.

(Remember, it wasn't the work or the occupation- it was the handful of evil bitches and the company that I was hating.) We were toasting Meesh, it had been her last day and I was sitting on a secret that I was going to sign my new contract for the new job over the weekend and then QUIT on Monday! There was good food, strong drinks and great friends I was going to miss but I knew that I was going to have to move on for my own peace of mind. Oh, and one of our friends is a chaplain so I felt as though I didn't really need to bring my filter.

#240 He was absolutely right; it wasn't me. It was him.

Remember Douche Bag who I kept whining about? Yeah, me too. Anyway, I wasn't remembering him quite so often and I wasn't whining about him in real life, either, at this point. However, when I got to the Caddyshack to meet my work friends the night before to toast Meesh and wish her well, guess who was there at another table having dinner with his new girlfriend? That's right! But that's not the best part: she has curly blonde hair and is a bit chubby. Hmmmm...who does that remind you of?

It was a bit of a sucker punch, for sure, to see that he wasn't kneeling on broken glass on naked knee beating his back with a leather whip for having screwed things up so badly with me that I had to dump him. (I already admitted I have a flare for the dramatic. Let it go.) I wisely pretended that I didn't notice him. I also pretended that I didn't see him staring at me. The next morning I woke up prepared to be all emotionally fucked up and what a pleasant surprise that instead I woke with the bit of clarity I wrote in my revelation.

It wasn't me. It was him. I dumped him and he went and found himself a new girlfriend who looks just like me. Good luck, girlfriend; you're going to need it.

#241

Emotional sucker punch+Xanax+Jello shots=do NOT text anyone who has seen you naked. just sayin'

I was over Douche Bag, pinky swear. I know you think I wasn't because I keep writing about him but honestly, seeing him with the Mia-look-alike at the bar gave me a real sense of closure. I was also over Heart Stomper. No, really, I was! I am! At this point, however, I was communicating with him quite a bit and we were doing an awful lot of wondering about what might have been. So, despite being over Douche Bag, seeing him was an emotional sucker punch that I medicated with Xanax and some Jello shots. *sigh* I'd like to renew my request for a breathalyzer on my blackberry, please.

Before you get too judgmental on me, however; let the record show that Heart Stomper is an active participant in this sick, twisted, little texting game and *he* is generally the one who crosses the line first. It's not like I don't jump right into that catapult with him to hurl ourselves across the line, but still. It takes two to tango and I really need to stop tangoing with him when I am altered.

#242

A change will do you good.

I did it! I quit the job!! Yes, I had signed my contract for the new job over the weekend and that Monday morning I walked into the director's office with my letter in my hand. I asked him, point blank, if I was going to be considered for the promotion I had my eye on. He hemmed and hawed and mumbled about how valuable I was in my current position, yada yada yada. I handed him my letter, told him my last day would be the following Friday and reminded him that the next day was a scheduled personal day off. Free at last, free at last, thank God almighty I was free at last!

August 31, 2010

#243

Go big or go home! I'm up in about an hour, lucky #95...

Do you know any of those people who watch tv and say shit like, "I could totally do that." Yeah, well, not only am I one of them when it comes to the Food Network I'm also one of those go for it, Carpe Diem gals! I posted this revelation from the hotel in Philly where I was preparing to audition for *The Next Food Network Star.*

September

20 years
Post-High School
Revelation

#244

The waiting is the hardest part.

Waiting to hear from the Food Network. Waiting to finish my sentence at the job I hated. Waiting for my life to begin. I totally get that the Universe will put the lessons and challenges in my path that I need to learn but come on already! Clearly I am a failure at waiting and patience. At some point the Universe is just going to have to give up on me, don't you think?

#245

I'm still waiting for the revelation that teaches me patience and how to "let go & let God." I'd like to learn that lesson NOW, please!

Thursday arrives and I'm still trudging to work and still waiting for the phone to ring. Damn you, Food Network! You're like a man. We had a terrific first date; you gave me every indication that you liked me as much as I liked you. You asked for my number and you still won't call! Maybe I should have put out.

#246

If you're having a day so shitty that you even go home early from work w/ a migraine and find the Patrick Swayze classic *Roadhouse* on TV then things start to look up.

Friday arrived and I was staring down the barrel of another week of work...puke. Truth be told, I was really hoping that the director was going to accept my resignation and hand me a box so I could pack up my desk. He didn't, dammit; instead he made me train my replacement. My body was cooperative where the company from hell was not. I went home with my migraine, using up my last few hours of sick time, and hit the couch to find a cheesy 80s classic on television. Nice.

#247

Power nap & a hot shower; it does a body good!

Migraine gone. Three-day weekend here. Date tonight. Life is good.

#248

Men don't actually want women to be honest.

Yeah, they say they want honesty but they don't. Not really. I had been out the night before on a first date with a match from an online dating site. Yeah, I *am* that desperate. He seemed like a decent guy, we had chatted a bit via e-mail, text and phone and agreed to meet for a drink which led to dinner and an altogether good time with decent conversation. Full disclosure: my profile on the site clearly states that yes, I want to have children. I realize I am rapidly running out of time so it's not something I'm willing to be very coy about. Well, in the course of the date and conversation, which was really nice, the subject of kids comes up and he tells me he doesn't want to have any more. I tell him that's a shame as I was beginning to like him. Does that mean I don't want to go out with him again, he wonders. I don't really see the point, I tell him. I want to have kids and you don't; why waste our time? He asks me, "You don't want to be friends?" I didn't turn to online dating for friends; I have lots of friends.

Can we just have sex, then?

Only if there's some sperm in it for me, buddy.

Buh-bye...

September 6, 2010

#249

Sleeping next to a 3-year-old is like sleeping in a small cage with a wild monkey on acid...

So my Sunday night turned out to be so much more fabulous than my Saturday night! My sister, her kids, my cousin and her husband came over for an impromptu bite to eat, witnessed my goldfish leap to her death onto the tile kitchen floor and then Ruben attempt life-saving CPR before we all walked a few blocks to watch the Labor Day fireworks. It was fun and casual and my niece and nephew, 5 and 3½, respectively, had a blast. After a five-block round-trip walk through the city and a good amount of running around the steps of the Capital while the grown-ups watched the display of lights, their flip-flops proved to be powerless against the filth and grime of downtown Harrisburg. They wanted to sleep over, which was cool, but there was no way they were putting those filthy feet on my clean sheets. A little foot bath in the kitchen sink and the three of us were off to snuggle and watch a movie in my bedroom. I was really looking forward to our sleepover. It had been a fun evening, I love spending uninterrupted time with them and there was a promise of pancakes in the morning. We had a tense little showdown when my cats realized that their bed had been occupied by tiny humans, but the felines took solace in taking over the two square feet I had carved out for myself and all was right with the world. The kids fell asleep rather quickly and I laid there next to them marveling at their preciousness.

And then it began.

Ben woke up and looked around in a panic, having briefly forgotten where he was. I reassured him and put him in the middle between Abby and me to go back to sleep. Ha! Ben is his mother's son, 100%. He tosses. He turns. He kicks, smacks, punches and hurls his body like a cannonball. Needless to say, when Zia got up at the butt-crack of dawn, she was not refreshed and eager to make pancakes. I took a shower and inhaled some coffee before I got the kids set up in front of Harry Potter and went into the kitchen to make their promised pancakes. Abercrombie, Bennerman; Zia loves you but from now on when you sleep over Ben gets his own bed!

September 7, 2010

#250

Situations are never hopeless; the way we mere mortals think and react to them, however, often is.

I had to give myself a little pep talk to go back to hell, I mean work.

September 8, 2010

#251

I love the color red, I mean really love it. It's totally my favorite. I hate orange. It makes me angry.

September 9, 2010

#252

In fact it IS possible for two people to consume 100 shrimp and all the trimmings in a single sitting!

I *finally* got released from my sentence at the company from hell and celebrated by having lunch with my bff at Red Lobster. We tested, and proved, our theory. I needed a nap after.

September 10, 2010

#253

There really, really needs to be a *The West Wing* reunion movie.

I woke up with no alarm and spent the morning lounging, watching reruns of *The West Wing* on Bravo. I miss that show. ☹

September 11, 2010

#254

Freedom is not free. Sadly, the price was paid with innocent lives 9 years ago today and events were set into motion to forever change the hearts and lives of the entire world. To my students @ CCHS who watched in horror with me as the second plane hit the second tower, I was praying with you even though I was forbidden to do so; I ♥ you still. God Bless America!

Barby, "So many of those lives were not even American ☹"

Mia, "It's true, Cugina; but sadly they died because they were friends of America and her freedom. I honor them and their sacrifice as one of our own. To shed their blood for our way of life makes them American, too. Their families tears are our tears, too. Our survival is their triumph, too."

Barby, "Do not be overcome by evil, but overcome evil with good."

#255

September 12, 2010

To win without honor is no victory.

The new NFL season arrived this weekend. Michael Vick had been named the starting quarterback of the Philadelphia Eagles. Now, everyone who knows me knows how much I love the Eagles. I always have; I bleed Eagle green! The year before, I was watching a pre-season game when I heard that the monster had been signed to my team. I turned off the game and vowed to sit the season out. I can't, in good conscience, be loyal to another team or shit on my team, but I feel so betrayed by them putting that monster on my team.

Side Note: before you get all indignant and start yelling at this book about he's paid his debt to society and what about the football players who have killed *people* let me remind you that this is my book. If you have something to say write your own! Also, yell all you want, the book is not going to answer.

So, I sat out last season and endured the pain of watching my quarterback get traded to Washington over the summer and the new season arrived with that monster not only firmly in place but in a position of honor. Bullshit. I call bullshit. He is a *monster*!! He does not deserve to be a member of an NFL team. I don't give two shits how talented he is and how many games he will help my Eagles win. To win without honor is no victory, dammit. As of the writing of this commentary, Vick is enjoying a renaissance of sorts. He's having a great season, he's gotten a ridiculous number of votes for the pro bowl and even the president took time out of his busy schedule of turning our country into the Socialist States of America to praise him. Once again, I call bullshit! No, no, no, no, no!!

Whether you want to be or not, professional athletes are role models and should be held to a higher moral standard. There are hundreds of almost-made-it athletes who would love to have the chance to run out onto that field every week. There are thousands of teens busting their asses to learn the game in high school in hopes of a college scholarship and maybe, just maybe, a chance to play professionally. There are millions of children looking at you. Be better.

Michael Vick went to college. He can get another job. Yes, he served his jail time but he absolutely, positively does not deserve the honor of being a professional athlete. Now, if he gets locked in a cage with an angry and scared pit bull with nothing more than a collar, his muscles and his instinct to protect and defend himself and he makes it out alive then maybe I'll forgive

him. However, he still does not deserve to be a professional
athlete. Period.

#256

**Don't post an opinion poll as your
facebook status unless you REALLY
want to know what people think!
(not complaining, just marveling at
the responses. Thanks, all!)**

My friend was having a little moral dilemma and asked
for my advice. I said, "Take it to facebook!" She didn't want to so
I did it on her behalf, anonymously. Wow. My friends certainly
came through with surprising speed and amazing insight. FYI,
here was the dilemma:

Mia Semuta is trying to help a friend with a moral dilemma. She
shares 50/50 custody with her ex-husband and he is currently
re-married to the woman with whom he had an affair leading to
their divorce. He'll be out of town for 3 weeks for work,
including 1 week that he should have the kids. Should she let
them go & be with the stepmother or no? The only reason we
can come up with is, "No, because she's a whore." Thoughts?

Forty-seven comments later, my friend talked to the kids
who were receptive to spending the week with stepmom who
was even more excited to get a whole week with the kids all to
herself. I recommended Xanax and wine to my friend. I think it
was easier for my friends to anonymously weigh the pros and
cons and offer their advice than for me because I kept coming
back to, "But she's a whore!!" She should burn in hell with
Michael Vick. What did we do before facebook?

#257

To witness wrong-doing and then to stand idly by and do nothing is just as much a sin as the bad deed itself.

Okay, get comfy because this is quite the tale to tell. I had been hating the job at evil company from hell. I found a new job that would utilize both my education and experience plus my sales skills as the Director of Marketing at an educational services company. Awesome! I quit hell and went over to my new gig on the previous Friday afternoon to check things out. Oh.My.God. In the three hours I spent there I noticed at least a dozen health and safety code violations. I still hold a license to teach from the Commonwealth of Pennsylvania. I'm not sure if I ever want to be a teacher again, but I'm certainly not going to risk it by ignoring these violations. Even if I didn't have something to lose, these codes exist for a reason and these children were in danger.

I tried to talk to my new boss about it and he brushed away my concerns. I went home at the end of the day and decided to take the weekend to sleep and pray on it. I went back on Monday morning and found that not only had none of the issues been addressed, they were escalating. Again, I went to my new boss with my concerns. He told me to, "Shut up, go make some coffee and do your fucking job." Well, alrighty then. That's the thing about prayer. Sometimes the answer comes in the most shocking of ways.

I went back to work on Tuesday because, quite frankly, I really needed the paycheck. However, while I was at work that day I called the Pennsylvania Department of Public Welfare and filed a complaint and then I called ABC 27 and *The Patriot News* to shine a little light on this nightmare. I also jetted out to an interview during my lunch break. I knew- without a doubt- that I could not stay at that job. I was just hoping to last the week and get a paycheck.

About 7:00 PM that night I got a call from the new boss. He fired me over the phone. Totally worth it, though. Keep reading...

#258
September 15, 2010

It's a beautiful day in the neighborhood!

Unemployment day #1. I lay on the couch surfing facebook and feeling sorry for myself most of the day despite my attempts to force myself out of the funk with a positive attitude and the revelation I chose for the day. I noticed a panicked post by a former student. She was in a pinch and needed child care for the next day. I thought to myself, "You seriously have nothing planned, Mia. You should go take care of Chloe." So, I responded and told her she could count on me the next morning and went back to my regularly scheduled sulking despite my efforts to console myself that I had done the right thing.

#259
September 16, 2010

Karma is a beautiful thing.

I got up in the morning, took a shower, got to my babysitting gig on time and enjoyed a lovely morning with a lovely little girl. Sincerely. She was a happy baby, slept well, ate well, enjoyed my singing so there's no accounting for her taste, but I sat on the floor and played with the baby and enjoyed myself. It was good therapy and I knew that her mommy needed the help. My being there meant she could be at work, relaxed, and know that her baby was in good, CPR-trained hands. I had already made the mental decision that I was not going to charge her anything for one morning of babysitting and to just do good for doing good's sake.

That's about the time when my phone rang.

Interview, the next day, at a new hospice. HALLAH! (that's a happy shout, for the unenlightened out there.) I won't make you wait for it- got the job. ☺ Of course drama follows me everywhere I go so it wasn't exactly smooth sailing at first, but more on that later.

September 17, 2010

#260

The cool kids at the time called us a "grand experiment." 223 years later, our Constitution sets the gold standard. USA...USA...USA!!!

Old habits of social studies' teachers die hard; September 17 is Constitution Day. America is advanced citizenship, my friends; it's not for by-standers.

September 18, 2010

#261

Parents who refuse to medicate their hyperactive spawn should do society a favor and STOP feeding them SUGAR! And, for the love of God, breed no more.

It was interesting to see the debate that was sparked by this revelation. I was just annoyed by a brat I had been forced to endure and wanted to bitch about it. It became a forum for parents, teachers and others with no direct contact with kids other than to be forced to endure others' kids to sound off and share their insight. For the record, I don't believe all kids need medication but ALL kids need boundaries and discipline and no kids need to be bribed with sugar and fast food. Come on, people. Be parents. You choose to bring them into the world, please also choose to not just phone it in when it comes to parenting.

September 19, 2010

#262

Aurgh, Talk like a Pirate Day makes me laugh!

September 20, 2010

#263

Joy, laughter and happiness as well as sorrow, tears and anger are all choices; I am choosing light over dark.

Being in a good mood is a choice. There are many days that I have to remind myself to choose to find something to be happy about. It's often easier to just let the sadness take over and overwhelm but that doesn't really help. It's important to recognize and feel the sadness but you can't let it win.

#264

September 21, 2010

Take pleasure in the details.

A few pleasurable details:

- The first chip out of the bag.
- When someone says, "God Bless You," after I sneeze.

- Being greeted at the door by my kitties.
- A really good parking space.
- Seeing a rainbow or shooting star.
- Finding a four-leaf clover.
- New socks when it's really cold.
- Catching *Groundhog Day* on TV.

September 22, 2010

#265

If I continue to spend energy thinking about anniversaries- both happy and sad- there will be no room on the calendar for new memories.

The thing about fighting against sadness is that you kind of have to do it constantly.

September 23, 2010

#266

The gift that grief gives us is that the bad pieces and hurt feelings fade away and we are left with only good memories and joy. Happy Birthday, Mom. ❤

My mom would have turned 64 on this day. She died in June 2007 from ALS, (Lou Gherig's Disease.) The worst part, for me, of losing my mom so young wasn't just that I became a 35-year-old orphan but that my mom and I never really got along well. We just didn't understand one another. If we had not been mother and daughter, I don't think we would have chosen each other as a friend. As if that weren't bad enough, we both wasted far too much time trying to change the other into the person we wanted her to be instead of just accepting who she was. The solace I can take is that three years after she died, I am often unable to remember why I was always so angry with her. I remember her laughter and her goofiness. I remember her soup and her comforting "jello water" when I was sick. I remember her excitement and her naiveté. It's a nice feeling; to have happy and warm thoughts about my mother. I'm sad that it took her death to find them, but I honor them by choosing to let the bad things fade away. If I ever get to have kids of my own, it'll be the happy memories I share about their Nana so that they can know her, too.

#267

You take the good, you take the bad, you take them both and there you have the facts of life. The facts of life...

So, I was enjoying the last lazy Friday of unemployment and trying to solve a dilemma I was having. Yes, of course I took it to facebook. Have you not been paying attention? I was very excited to have been offered the job at the new hospice just one business day after my interview and I eagerly accepted it. Of course, in the lag time between having been offered the job and my start date a week later, I interviewed for a second job at a different company! As my friends, Lacy and Megan, pointed out: I was a total failure at unemployment. I had already contacted the HR rep at the new hospice where I was due to start working on Monday. She had advised me to speak to the regional manager who would be in the office on my start date. Okay, fine, good advice. But that leaves me the *entire* weekend to wonder. I think we've already established how horrible I am at waiting and what a tough time I have with patience. *sigh*

September 25, 2010

#268

I refuse to be a slave to the clock; just had chicken bites & a cup of coffee for breakfast. ☺

It was tasty. I dunked the chicken in Caesar dressing and put French Vanilla in my coffee. ☺

September 26, 2010

#269

Faith is not the absence of doubt; it's the will to keep moving forward without any proof.

Sunday arrived with my having no idea if I would be offered the second job at the new company or if the new hospice would tell me to go jump in a lake instead of starting there. I just had no idea and I had to breathe in and breathe out anyway. I had a feeling that I would come to the following Sunday with a firm offer of a good job that I really wanted, but I had absolutely no evidence. This, my friends, is faith.

September 27, 2010

#270

Rainy Mondays are manageable only with chocolate.

Of course it's raining the day I go for orientation at the new hospice! Rainy days and Mondays, aurgh. Let me bring you up to speed a bit. The new hospice did not have an opening in their marketing department when I interviewed. They had a secretarial position open and since I was unemployed when they offered it to me I took it. I really like working for hospice because it's a service I believe in and if I can't use the experience

I have with grief to help others then why the hell did I have to cry so much? Well, the other company was making a really attractive offer so even though it was not in hospice, I couldn't say "no" to what they were offering if there was no opening for me in the marketing department at the hospice. I spoke to the regional manager when I got to work that day and she set up a phone interview for me the next day with the Corporate Marketing Director. They came to play. Naturally, I got a call from the other company during the course of the day to sweeten the offer and to come in for a final interview the next day. When I got home, I took it straight to facebook:

Mia Semuta is in a quite a quandary, a downright pickle. Two jobs on the table, final interviews for each tomorrow, here's the skinny: Job A wins on perks, room for advancement, $$ and soul-satisfaction. Job B wins on insurance, retirement plan, ease and opportunity to travel. The hours are equally bad for both. Help me, facebook; you're my only hope...

Naturally, facebook came through in an amazing way!

Lora "Can you take the extra $$ from Job A and invest on your own for retirement? Soul-satisfaction is of primary importance IMHO - if you can at least live comfortably on Job A's income."

Amanda "You're young to be planning for retirement but insurance is a plus with this economy. But soul satisfaction would win me over. Which would you be happier with and less stressed?? How are your Co workers? You have to like who you work with and work for. If I win the lotto I would hire you as a cook/nanny!!! The kids would love that!"

Mia "It is more than likely I'll be offered both but not very likely I'll be responsible enough to invest on my own. Both start about the same time, B is more stable but less exciting. A is more satisfying but possible I'll not do as well, ergo, maybe not get to keep it."

Mia "Amanda, when you win I'll take the job!! Co-workers equal @ both, I'm not too young to think retirement, Cugina. I'm pushing 40 in the express lane! Equal stress."

Amanda "You're too funny Mia! I hope your choice works out great for you!!!"

John "In this economy go for stability."

Shannon "whats your gut feeling? obviously you can make it by on the income of both or both would not be an option. How much would it cost to get insurance privately? Factor that cost in and subtract it from the income of the first job and if you can still make ends meet then I would go with the job I would be HAPPY and satisfied with."

Kelly "Job A would include travel, 401K for benes and has good insurance also. But its very challenging and a very new arena for you. Are you up for that kind of position or would you be more inclined to stick with what you know. That's the real question. "

Nicole "I say go for A, you'd get bored not having a challenge. As for the retirement, you could always set up a direct withdrawal with the bank into an IRA. And they probably do offer insurance at job A, but didn't want to tell you about the boring stuff."

Mia "I would be good at both, would enjoy both, B would be easier, A would be more challenging/scary."

Scott "soul satisfaction the entire way!!!"

Scott "travelling for work isn't the same as vacationing unless you can share it with family/friends"

Lacy "Kelly makes the most logical sense to I'm just going to ditto what she says. At the end of the day you need insurance so if the cost of private insurance still makes A a better bet then go for it."

Ted "Coin flip is your only best option here."

Mia "Thanks, Ted. ☺ I was afraid of that. I'm kind of hoping I only get offered one so I don't have to decide. Oh, Job A gives me the chance to really stick it to someone I can't stand!!"

Barby "Opportunity to travel where? You know I ask only because my last job always had me traveling to Houston in August and Denver in November. LOL. Muta, you could excel at any job you set your mind too. What does your heart tell to you choose? If it is A, there are ways to supplement insurance (I am guessing you refer to health insurance) and save for retirement. BTW, in this economy you are NEVER too young ☺ Let us know if we can help in any way and good luck with your decision. ♥ U! xo"

Mia "The thing is that when I inhale I want A, when I exhale I want B. :-/ I know I'll do well at both, travel to training centers all over the country & Puerto Rico. I have friends everywhere and the job is so second nature to me that it would be able to visit & vacay on the company dime. But I can't be too creative with B. A let's me be my full on ME, but much harder. Seriously, I can go either way on this."

Ted "Oh, then Job A it is. Wait, unless that person is ME! ☺"

Donna "'Sticking it to someone' would probably be temporarily satisfying, so that probably appeals to you, but I agree with Barby and say choose the one your heart calls you to. It sounds on the surface that A would be the better choice but you ...know your own financial situation and comfort level. Think about this: where would you WANT to be, career-wise in 10 years. Which of these jobs would get you there? PS What happened to the job you were supposed to start today?"

Lisa "have you had firm offers on both?"

Mia "I started today, Donna. Job A is a promotion at that company that is on the table now that I've told them I'm considering Job B. My heart and cat-like reflexive decision making is annoyingly silent at the moment. Dammit."

Mia "No, Lisa; final interviews for both tomorrow. All indicators point to two firm offers."

Donna "Ohhhhh. OK, I was concerned that today's job had fallen through. But if Job A offered a promotion only because they heard about Job B, I'd wonder why I wasn't offered Job A in the first place. Anyway... I'll pray for your insight to return. Take a breath. Change is scary and either way you'll have to walk by faith."

Sue "Take the one that gives you the soul satisfaction. You know that's the one you really want and you're definitely getting verification from your friends and family. You know you'll be happier...and happiness is 100% worth it."

Ruth "I think I'd go with A, and use the extra $ for insurance and to set up my own retirement plan. It sounds more challenging and therefore you are less apt to get bored with the job. The more you push yourself, the better chance you have to impress the powers that be. In job B, it sounds as if you would be coasting along, so you'd likely lose interest relatively quickly and not put forth your full effort out of sheer boredom, but that's JMHO."

Susan "Well I suggest you do what you find most satisfying, Sounds like Job A and as far as insurance and retirement, there are good places to get advice and set up with the right coverage for you. I can recommend some if you would like. So my best advice, is relax, breathe deep and let your mind clear and you will have your answer. ☺"

Mia "I think I'm thinking too hard! I'll sleep on it and wait for divine intervention, thanks all for the insight & advice. ☺"

John "If you can get $$ and soul satisfaction in the same job then that is the one you should take. It's a rare combination."

James "Soul satisfaction versus ease? The unchallenged life is not worth living."

Michael "I've got to agree with John, if you can get all that AND room for growth I say go for it. Now, of course, take the job you are offered."

John "Clearly, Michael is a wise man. As for James, very profound. An unchallenged Mia would not be the Mia I know."

Matt "The extra $$ from job A can be put into a retirement fund."

Karolyn "Seems like a VERY tough decision!! (And sorry I'm so late on this) But I think I would have to go with A. As sad as it is to say, in this economy: NO ONE is "stable" in their job. I've known several people who've been working for companies 10 years+, and lost their jobs. It's a shame. But A sounds more exciting, and it DEFINITELY seems to fit you better, Muta!!! But I'm sure God and your heart will push you in the right direction, and it will all work out amazing!! Love you!!!!!! ps: I'm slooooooooooooooowly reading those books. Hahaha"

September 28, 2010

#271 **Clarity usually arrives when I'm right in the middle of something else.**

My mind was totally wrapped up in the job quandary. I thought I knew what I wanted but the more I thought about it the more confused I got! I was still thinking, hoping, praying, reading facebook...

Mia Had a great interview w/ Job A, think they'll make a sweet offer tomorrow. Just had my interview w/ Job B, they want me to come back to give a presentation. I think an offer is forthcoming there as well. I woke up this morning and I knew I wanted Job B, but Job A is going to offer first. I could really use a good distraction!! ☺

#272

When it comes to relationships and matters of the heart, we're all still only 16-years old.

I took a short break from obsessing about the job to go back to my default obsession: men. September 29 is a special day for me and a certain someone but I'm keeping it to myself. ☺ Some things are too precious to exploit. However, news on this day from the job front...

Mia Firm offer from Job A, I countered with two minor things that aren't at all deal-breakers just to stall for time. Not gonna lie, feels pretty good to be wanted!

#273

There is no such thing as coincidence.

By mid day, Job B had not returned my phone call to schedule my presentation nor had they made a firm offer. However, Job A had come back to me and met my two counter-offers. I decided to do what most of my friends had been encouraging me to do all along: I went with my gut and accepted the offer. ☺ My secretarial career lasted all of three days. Later that day, when I finally got a call from Job B to schedule my presentation I told them that I had accepted the other position. You snooze, you lose. No, I didn't really say that last bit out loud but I did think it!

20 years
Post-High School
Revelation

#274

I really don't know how much wood a woodchuck would chuck if a woodchuck could chuck wood and quite frankly, I don't really give a damn!

WOOT! I was in such a good mood I didn't care about anything! ☺ It felt awesome to have a job and I was totally at peace with my decision. The thing about feeling too good about yourself is that something will always come along and put things into perspective.

Kim / Kimberly "Damn? Shouldn't that be I don't give a fuck? It rhymes!!"

Fuck. How did I miss that?

Moving on, I posted this to put an end to the job dilemma:

Mia Good morning! In case you missed it yesterday, I've chosen Job A. ☺ I will be the new Community Education Representative, (CER), at a Hospice. I had also been courted as a corporate trainer for an insurance company, but after all the negotiations and debate, working for and with patients and their families as they come to the end of life's journey is what called to me the most. Thank you all for your good vibes and advice!

#275

Thank God for lazy days of no alarms, flexible plans and deadlines written in pencil.

#276

Movies in 3-D freakin' rule!

The night before I took Abby and Ben to see *Alpha and Omega* in 3-D. I'll admit that I was feeling so relieved and at peace that my work crap was all settled that I wasn't feeling overly inspired in the revelation arena. This was a stretch. I phoned this one in from the movie theatre. Oh, what? What's that? You're disappointed? Well get over it and write your own freakin' revelation every day for an entire freakin' year! It's not as easy as you think. Damn, everyone's a critic.

#277

Chance late night phone calls and cool autumn weather, homemade mac & cheese and soft fuzzy sweaters, sweet-talking liars who say, "I love how you sing." These are a few of my favorite things!

Now, go back and re-read that to the tune of the *Sound of Music* song and you'll have a little glimpse inside my head.

#278

You can spend a lifetime trying to make everyone happy only to spectacularly fail and yet you can piss of the entire world without even trying!

That's how I like my irony served.

#279

Seriously, I could sell ice to an Eskimo; honey to a bee.

Nine days on the new job and I signed a patient. Sweet! I resisted the urge to call the old boss and the vicious bitch at the job in hell and rub it in. I'm certain that the grapevine was quite effective. In fact I'm certain of it because she un-friended me on facebook shortly thereafter. Boo-fuckin'-hoo...

#280

Don't go for second best, baby, put your love to the test. (thanks, Madonna ☺)

You know, you know, you know you've got to make him express how he feels and baby then you know your love is real!

#281

Some people and situations come into our lives for the sole purpose of putting our egos on a diet.

It's important to be taken down a peg now and then. It keeps you motivated.

October 9, 2010

#282

I'm through accepting limits 'cause someone says they're so. (thank you, Wicked ☺)

Yeah, I may be taken down a peg now and then and I'm grateful for it but don't think for one second I'm not taking back three pegs for every one taken from me. ☺

October 10, 2010

#283

There is meaning and significance in everything the Universe throws at you. Today, on 10/10/10, I sure would love a little Cliff's Notes to go with it!

I swear this is not just another phoned in revelation because I was struggling. I really did feel as though there was something I should be understanding about the day but I had no freakin' clue what it was.

October 11, 2010

#284

Ignorance + Misplaced Shame = Hurting the people best equipped to help.

My friend was having a real tough time and I was powerless to help. That's called frustration.

#285

October 12, 2010

Putting on Spanx is a freakin' workout.

Quit laughing and go get some Spanx. You'll see what I mean.

#286

October 13, 2010

I don't get nearly enough sleep.

#287

October 14, 2010

I am so fortunate to live in the North East; the fall colors are breath-taking.

I hear people singing the praises of San Diego and Florida and blah blah blah. Whatever, keep your humidity and heat all year 'round. I'll take the change of seasons and the breathtaking views that the North East gives me when I look around my hometown.

#288

October 15, 2010

Love should be multiplied not divided. (Not sure I agree with your lifestyle, Kody Brown, but I love your theory!)

I don't think I could ever be a sister-wife, (I don't share well), but I do love the thought that love should be multiplied.

#289

October 16, 2010

Your body's internal clock is only reliable on holidays and weekends.

Wide awake at 6:00 AM on a Saturday morning. Dammit.

#290

October 17, 2010

Just because we disagree doesn't mean one of us is wrong.

I think this has been one of the hardest lessons to learn. Once I did, however, it brought such a lovely sense of peace. It's more than just agreeing to disagree; it's about accepting that sometimes there is no resolution or correct answer and that's okay.

#291

October 18, 2010

NyQuil is a recreational drug.

It should also be a valid defense in a court of law. just sayin'

#292

October 19, 2010

Seriously, I can really cook.

No, seriously. I can. You want proof? My friend, Megan, and I won a Chili Cook off tonight. BAM!

Six Million Dollar Chili
Winner of the 2010 HBA of Metro Harrisburg
5th Annual Chili Cookoff

Marinade:
Fresh juice of 3 limes
12 oz jar of pickled jalapenos (brine included)
4 oz olive oil
1 pack of taco seasoning
2 tsp. ground fresh chili paste
4 tsp. minced garlic
1 tsp. wasabi paste
¼ cup Sriracha
2 long john peppers- seeds and ribs included
12oz. Olive Oil

Combine the above in a blender on purée and liquefy. Add an additional 12 oz olive oil and wisk gently. Pour into a vacuum sealable bag with 2 pieces Top Round London Broil, seal and refrigerate for 24-48 hours.

Chili:
Butter (2 sticks)
Onions (2 whole)
Bell peppers (6 red and green)
Carrots (1 bag shredded, chopped)
Kosher salt (1/8 cup)
Flour (1 cup)
Corona (2-3 bottles depending on desired thickness)
Hot Spiced Oil (from marinade)
Chili pepper paste (2 oz)
Cilantro paste (2 oz)
Corn (3 cans, drained)
Tomatoes (3 cans whole crushed with liquid)
Tomatoes (6 Roma, cut into small chunks)
Sazón (2 packets)
Banana Peppers with brine (16 oz)

Black beans (4 cans, drained)
Sriracha (3 T)
Chili powder (1 T)

Remove the Steak from the marinade and grill until Medium rare, reserve the marinade. After the meat rests, cut into very small bite-sized pieces. Set aside.

Place the leftover marinade in a saucepan and bring slowly to a boil, stirring frequently. Allow to boil at least 3 minutes. The oil will rise to the surface. Pour off the oil and reserve to be added to the chili, discard the remaining.

Sautée the Onions, Bell Peppers and Carrots in the Butter with the Kosher Salt until lightly caramelized. Add the flour and then Corona to make a roux. Simmer gently adding the Hot Spiced Oil a little at a time. Add the Chili Pepper Paste and Cilantro Paste, continue to simmer. Add the Corn, Canned Tomatoes, Fresh Tomatoes, Black Beans and Banana Peppers, continue to simmer. Finally, add the Sriracha, Chili Powder and meat. Simmer for as long as you can stand not having a bowl!

October 20, 2010

#293 The only way to change is one step at a time; and every single step matters.

New job was fantastic! I was doing the job that I wanted to do in the industry I wanted to be in but my poor little office was in a state of flux. There had been some turmoil and some upheaval, a bit of a ba-rue-ha-ha, if you will. I was determined to help turn it around but the task just seemed daunting. I had to take a moment to remind myself that I just had to start somewhere and have a little faith.

#294

Damn, it feels good to be a gangsta...

HIPPA laws and just good morals prevent me from explaining in detail but suffice it to say that not only was I finding success in my new job I was also sticking it to the vicious bitch from the job in hell. Woo-Hoo!!

#295

Be nosey, be a pest, tattle; do whatever it takes to get the help that's needed for the people you love. Not one more needs to ever slip away in the night feeling lonely and hopeless. Not one more. ♥

I'm often asked why I left teaching. It was a combination of reasons, honestly, but the final straw for me was losing a student to suicide. He was just sixteen-years-old and found himself in a state of mind that he thought hopeless and he chose to end it. He didn't ask for my help and I don't know if I would have been able to if he had, but the pain that I had to both witness and bare was just more than I could continue to burden myself with so I left my career and embarked on a myriad of others. Anyway, many of the kids that I had as students have become friends of mine both on facebook and in real life.

On this day I was thinking of my student who had slipped away in the night four years prior and the words I had spoken at a candle-light vigil for him a few days after his death came to mind. I was not supposed to encourage or endorse any sort of memorial among the kids, as directed by the powers-that-be at the school where I taught; I most certainly was not supposed to organize the thing and supply the candles. But, I did because in my heart I knew that somebody needed to give these kids a place to gather and share their grief and *somebody* had to say out loud, "This is not an option. Don't do it." I had been powerless to help one but I was not about to stand idly by and do nothing for the rest.

I organized a candle-light vigil at 9:00 PM at a local, public park. I got the word out by quietly telling key members of different groups of friends and making them promise to keep my name out of it. I bought the candles and stayed up all night cutting blue ribbon to make memorial pins. As I sat on my bed doing that I cried; I prayed for the strength and for the words that I would need to get through to the rest of my kids that they needed to survive this. Suicide is contagious and I was determined to do everything in my power to make my kids immune to it. The night of the memorial I lit candles and I pinned ribbons on jackets and I stood on a table to talk to my kids knowing that if I got "caught" I may be fired from my job. I remember one of the kids calling out to me, "Muta, are we allowed to swear?"

"Baby," I replied, "you say whatever the fuck you want just promise me that you'll keep talking."

It got a laugh and their attention and that's when I told them not one more. Not one more time do we gather and say goodbye to a friend too soon. Not one more of them needs to feel helpless and hopeless. Not one more night needs to be spent without anyone to turn to. Not one more. It became the refrain I hoped it would. For the rest of the year at school I saw kids wearing the blue ribbon and I wore mine on my name tag until it frayed beyond recognition. It's in my jewelry box now and I see it every day and I think of the smiling, happy kid who preferred to sit on the table and put his feet on the wall rather than sit in a chair to learn Civics. I remember that it's important to butt in, to be nosey, to be a pest and to tattle.

I also think how glad I am that I took the chance and brought a few hundred of my kids and a handful of their parents together that night. It was the beginning of the end for me as a teacher because I knew I couldn't go back to an institution that would frown upon what I had done. And I think about my friends and me, when we were just kids, gathering at a funeral for one of our own because he had taken his life. Everything happens for a reason. I had fulfilled my destiny as a teacher after ten years when I was able to tell my kids not one more. The only reason I was able to do that effectively is because I had walked where they were walking and I had felt their pain and I had cried their tears. I was able to help my kids survive that which seemed impossible because my friends and I had survived it, too. And so my work there was done.

October 23, 2010

#296 Sadly, there is no pill or therapy to fix stupid.

Trust me, I was a teacher for a long time and I know from stupid.

October 24, 2010

#297 Challenges keep me on my toes but overcoming them makes me hold my head up high.

I think I'd be bored if I lived on Easy Street. Frankly, I have very little respect for those who do.

October 25, 2010

#298

Happiness is going out for wings with Megan because she likes the flats and I like the drummies. ☺

This one created quite a stir. Who knew that so many people had such strong opinions about hot wings?!

October 27, 2010

#299

Cults are both time consuming and pricey.

I had missed the day before because I was swamped and I had nothing significant to say. It's interesting that I didn't think much of it on the missed day but how perfect because events would occur on the next day that gave me a reason to need to write two. Anyway, there was this cult I had to join for work and it occurred to me that morning that I was not much of a follower and I had little patience for the indoctrination. I de-programmed myself two weeks later.

October 27, 2010

#300

To everything there is a season and a time for every purpose under heaven.

So I had just been giggling to myself about my previous revelation when I got word that my cousin's son had passed away. He was only twelve, had battled cancer for some time and God just decided that he had battled long enough. Once again, I found myself helpless and without much to give my cousin for her pain or to give myself for my own. It is my faith that there is, certainly, a time for every season that pulls me through even that which seems to be insurmountable.

October 28, 2010

#301

Sometimes it's okay to be a follower if you have a really good leader. Heavenly Father, walk through my home and take away all of my worries and any illnesses and please watch over and heal my family and friends in Jesus name, Amen. This prayer is so powerful. Stop what you're doing & set this to your status. Watch what God will do.

I was again reminded of divine timing when I saw this prayer as someone's status and I thought that maybe it's okay to be a follower and copy someone else if their words and deeds are worthy of such an honor.

October 29, 2010

#302

Where necessity is the mother of invention passion is the mother of success.

Love, love, loving the job; feeling supremely frustrated with the challenge. Time to get creative.

#303 The greatest luxury on earth is freedom.

That's why it's so expensive. I'm not just talking about the monetary value of expense. Freedom takes its toll on the heart and soul, too. It's expensive and it's trying and it's painful. We take it for granted so often and so rarely stop to even say thank you to those who have paid our bill.

#304 You say you're only going out for one drink but add a pair of leopard ears and the next thing you know Mickey Mouse is slipping you the tongue, you've drunk dialed your past and you're crawling in bed @ 4 AM.

Okay, so I love Halloween. I really do. And I have this friend that really likes to be a bad influence. Don't feel too sorry for me, I'm totally a willing participant in the debauchery that follows, but still. It's his fault. I was just going to go to bed early and plan strategy for some other things I had going on when he called and said get ready, we're going out. Dammit. Okay. One. I'll go out with you for one drink. One. Yeah right, famous last words.

The revelation is completely accurate; to the best of my recollection. A peak at my phone the next, sober-ish morning confirmed that Heart Stomper was on the other end of the drunk-dialed phone. I know, you're thinking, "This has disaster written all over it."

You have no idea.

20 years
Post-High School
Revelation

#305

When in doubt, convene a secret panel to examine the situation.

I've tried a few different dating websites with varying degrees of success. I'm banned for life from eHarmony because we had a fundamental difference of opinion on the definition of "appropriate pictures" but that's an entirely different book. The day I had this revelation I was really trying to talk myself into liking this man I had been matched with on a free site.

Side Note: Let's take a moment to recall a favorite revelation of my Dad's: You get what you pay for.

Anyway, I wanted to like him. I really did. He was a nice guy, had come through in a very gentlemanly way when I was having a tough time of it, he was really tall and he was into me.

Another Side Note: Yes, I am well aware that if you have to convince yourself to like someone then it's probably a lost cause.

In my effort to talk myself into him I challenged him to a chili cook off. I was still high on my award winning performance with my friend, Megan, and he was talking a big pile of smack about how good his chili was. I also invited a bunch of my friends over to eat the chili with the understanding that this was a clandestine audition for the Tall Guy. In the end, I put on my big girl panties and cancelled the whole shebang because the truth was that no matter what my friends would have had to say I just didn't like him. The night of the cancelled chili cook off I planned to snuggle up with a movie on HBO but guess who called me and talked me into going downtown? That's right! My buddy from #304 and he brought a friend. I know, once again you're thinking, "This has disaster written all over it."

You still have no idea.

#306

Decisions are made by those who show up. VOTE! (And please vote right...)

Hey, do you know what happens the first Tuesday following the first Monday in November here in the USA? That's right! It's Election Day! Let it be known that I played my part in the new revolution. My, oh my, it sure was nice to wake up the next day to find Pennsylvania wearing red. ☺

#307

It's okay to ask God why; it's not okay to argue with the answer.

My cousin, Megan, and I were chatting a bit on facebook. She has such a strong faith and was handling the death of her son with amazing strength and grace but she was having a tough moment. As I sat at the keyboard doing my best to hug her through the screen I reassured her that it was perfectly normal to question God. God gave us the gift of higher thinking so we would question and wonder. However, that gift also came with the burden of not being able to argue if we didn't like what we heard. It's painful and frustrating, but it is what it is.

#308

Love yourself and all the good in you; others will feel it and love you, too.

I have this deck of spirituality cards that I keep on the book case in my bedroom. Most days I shuffle and choose one, asking for some guidance for the day. Every now and then, I get something that just blows me away with its appropriateness and insight. I pulled this particular one on this Thursday morning and it gave me the nudge I needed to cancel the chili sham date with the Tall Guy.

#309 You can't get mad at a leopard for having spots.

Cats chase mice, dogs bark at squirrels, birds shit on statues and men take to their assorted forms of technology to communicate with the owners of hearts they've stomped on when they're feeling a little low in the self-esteem department. Getting pissed and trying to change them will only give you grey hair and wrinkles.

#310 It's a good thing I can't check the balance on my Karma savings account because I would be spending it hand over fist being mean to the little rats at the mall!

Have I mentioned how much I hate shopping?

November 7, 2010

#311

The best days, making of the greatest memories, can't be planned; if you're lucky you're paying attention when they happen. ☺

The previous day was supposed to have been the grand chili cook off but instead I spent it shopping and lunching with my girl, Megan, and then boozing and scheming with my boys, Mike and Tommy. That shit can't be planned. Seriously, when the bandwagon comes along be ready for it, jump on and go for the ride!

November 8, 2010

#312

The best antidote for anger is love.

I know, I know, I know…you want to fight fire with fire and serve up some revenge but seriously, the only way to conquer anger is to love it more than it hates you.

November 9, 2010

#313

All we have to see is that I don't belong to you and you don't belong to me; yeah, yeah…Freedom!! (thank you, George Michael!)

iPod inspiration comes through in a big, big way! Heart Stomper was pretty heavy on my mind as we'd been communicating quite a lot lately and a reunion after nineteen years was imminent. Throw in a little 80s theme music and an entire movie montage played out in my head as I walked along the river.

#314

I love pie; especially apple. With ice cream. I don't love to make pie because rolling pie dough sucks, but I sure do love it when someone else makes it then it's a little slice of heaven.

This was revelation #314 and if you can't make the connection between my pie adoration and the number 314 then I need you to seriously reconsider your purchase of this book... Oh, and be jealous. I went to see Bret Michaels at the Forum that night. Rock of love, baby; rock of love!

#315

Like the knife that cuts you the wound heals, but that scar; that scar remains. Yes, I too am thinking about Veteran's Day, but the concert last night made me get pop-glam-rock-introspective. Many of our freedoms come with scars for those who have fought for it and for those who love them. Thank you, one and all, for all that we have. God Bless you and God Bless America!!

#316

Regret and sorrow can tear your soul apart if you let it; joy and gratitude can make you whole.

Kelly, "Gratitude is the spiritual equivalent of Prozac."

#317

Indeed, variety is the spice of life. I'm dedicating today's revelation to the fabulously eclectic band of merry-makers that make up my circle. I am surrounded by laughter and love daily from an amazing variety of genres and I wouldn't have it any other way! ❤

For no particular reason I just felt like appreciating my friends and family today. ☺

November 14, 2010

#318

The Universe puts people in your life to teach you certain lessons; some as an example of how to be and others as a cautionary tale. The challenge we all face is to understand and sort them appropriately.

The lessons are all around you. Nobody passes through your life for no reason; even if you wish they hadn't bothered. There's something to learn from all of them.

November 15, 2010

#319

A day spent without having done something that terrifies you is a day wasted.

I'm not entirely certain what a laurel is but I do know that I'll never, ever, be content to rest on them.

November 16, 2010

#320

I am still trying to be the person my pets think I am.

When I was nineteen I foolishly married my first husband, Rebound. Shortly after our wedding, he was off with the Army and I was basically a single girl in my hometown with a new last name and a fake ID, (Rebound wrote down the wrong birth date for me on my Department of Defense ID paperwork and as it made me twenty-one well before my time, I failed to point out the error.) Eight months into our marriage I was out of excuses for not moving to where he was and I packed up and moved to

Kansas. Can you say miserable? Especially when I found out he would be leaving once again for thirty days only a month after I got there. Yep, I was pissed. He consoled me by taking me to Oklahoma to buy me a dog. I wanted a German Shepherd so off we went to Tulsa to a breeder's farm to choose a dog.

This was a beautiful facility. They bred only German Shepherds and the dogs had pristine living conditions so I knew it was going to cost a lot of money but I was going to be alone in Kansas, dammit, and I didn't really want to be married to him anyway so I wasn't too concerned about how much he would be spending on my dog.

There was a huge, fenced-in area where there were approximately fifty dogs playing and being socialized. The first part of our tour took us past this play yard. The owner of the farm used his fingers to make one of those loud whistles I always wished I knew how to do and a dozen dogs came running over to us at the fence. One of them, an eight-month old female, ran right up to me, stood on her hind legs and put her paws on the fence where I was standing. Ours eyes connected and I said, "Here she is. This is my dog."

Rebound wanted to look around some more and the owner was eager to show off his beautiful facility. I didn't mind the tour, but I knew who was coming home with me. She trotted along beside us everywhere we went and after an hour they were convinced of what I knew in the first minute. Peyton Louise piled into the car with us for the five-hour drive back to Ft. Riley. She was mine, through and through.

After nearly eleven years and two husbands, my dear, sweet girl had finally had enough of this world. I had to become the protector and let her go. On November 16, 2002 she went to the Rainbow Bridge and I adopted her little brothers six months later. If someday I can be the person they think I am I will, without a doubt, be someone to look up to. I don't know who wrote this poem but it has most certainly helped me when I was crying myself into a puddle as I missed my baby girl.

The Rainbow Bridge

Just this side of heaven is a place called Rainbow Bridge. When an animal dies that has been especially close to someone here, that pet goes to Rainbow Bridge. There are meadows and hills for all of our special friends so they can run and play together. There is plenty of food, water and sunshine and our friends are warm and comfortable.

All the animals who had been ill and old are restored to health and vigor. Those who were hurt or maimed are made whole and strong again, just as we remember them in our dreams of days and times gone by. The animals are happy and content, except for one small thing; they each miss someone very special to them, who had to be left behind.

They all run and play together, but the day comes when one suddenly stops and looks into the distance. Her bright eyes are intent. Her eager body quivers. Suddenly she begins to run from the group, flying over the green grass, her legs carrying her faster and faster.

You have been spotted, and when you and your special friend finally meet, you cling together in joyous reunion, never to be parted again. The happy kisses rain upon your face; your hands again caress the beloved head and you look once more into the trusting eyes of your pet, so long gone from your life but never absent from your heart.

Then you cross Rainbow Bridge together.

November 17, 2010

#321

Sometimes I have to kiss a little ass and sometimes someone has to kiss mine; I much prefer being kissed...

I'm in sales.

November 18, 2010

#322

I firmly believe that meat grows on the Styrofoam trays under plastic wrap at the grocery store. Ergo, the sight of the beheaded deer in the back of the pickup truck was soooo not welcome!

It sucked big time. I had a salad for dinner.

November 19, 2010

#323

The entire world is mental.

I'm a Harry Potter fanatic and I don't care who knows it. I didn't get into the books when they first came out, but the first movie got me hooked on the story and I read the first four books in a weekend. Then, I had to wait over a year for the fifth book to come out. When I found out that it would be released in England three days before it was due to be released here, I planned my summer vacation around being in London that day. Oh yeah, I did. I tell you this so that you'll understand why I benched myself from all facebook activities from midnight the night before until the writing of this revelation.

The seventh movie, which is really the first part of the seventh book, was released at midnight. Quite a few of my facebook friends are also HP fans and I didn't want to be unduly influenced by their commentary before I went to see the movie at 7:00 PM with my cousin who was, ironically, coming in from London that day. I had purchased our tickets weeks before and we were eagerly anticipating the movie. I knew something would happen to inspire my revelation. I was right. Ron Weasley came through with the perfect quote, "The entire world is mental." It's so true and sadly, I was bitterly disappointed with the movie. ☹ It was nothing more than a 2½-hour preview for the second part due out in 2011. What a wasted opportunity, Warner Brothers.

November 20, 2010

#324 Sometimes I build walls just to see who is strong enough to knock them down.

As of this writing I am still single so clearly my strong man has yet to penetrate my defenses. The end credits are *not* rolling so I encourage all would-be suitors to please, for the love of God, ***please***, keep trying! You can often create a weak spot in the wall with a little Cap'n. just sayin'

November 21, 2010

#325 The scan is better than the pat down unless the TSA agent is Duane "The Rock" Johnson. In that case; yes, please, may I have a private room? ☺

Everybody was all wound up about the security measures at the airports. Gimme a fuckin' break! Is having your bod xrayed and the image shown in another room really worse than planes flying into buildings? Get some perspective, you dick-licking assholes! *Nobody* said you had to fly. If you don't want to do whatever it takes to keep us all safe then get the hell off of my airplane.

#326

Hot damn! Bargains are sexy!!

Still hate shopping, but I do love a bargain. It's a vicious, ironic twist, isn't it?

#327

Women plan, Mother Nature laughs; that bitch has one hell of a twisted, sick sense-of-humor.

My 20-year high school reunion was coming up in three days and I had two, count 'em, *two* dates. But what did I get *today* as a little extra bonus? Oh, the ladies know. I sure as hell did! I guess it was Mother Nature's way of saying, "No, no, Mia; no, no. You will not be a filthy little whore this weekend. Now, go get some chocolate covered pretzels and put on your sweat pants." I hate that bitch.

#328

Death takes no holidays. Cross gently and rest in peace Aunt Mary. ♥

And just when I got myself good and wrapped up in my own shit, my Gramma's sister passed away quietly in her sleep. She and Gramma were the last of thirteen with ten surviving to adults. Aunt Mary was ninety-five and loved to read my books—even the spicy ones! I was so very glad that I was able to spend time with her at the reunion this past summer but my heart was so broken for my Gramma as she had to say goodbye to her sister and know that she is the last of her family still here on this side. Sweet dreams, Aunt Mary; until we meet again.

#329

You can cry a river with sadness but if you learn from them, your tears can build a bridge across that river. I am thankful for every experience the Universe has given me; the good and the bad. I am thankful that I woke up today with a new chance to find joy and to share it. Happy Thanksgiving! ♥

When I am right in the middle of a painful lesson it's really hard to be thankful for it, but taking the time to remind myself and being consciously grateful helps to make the pain pass much quicker.

#330

Happiness often sneaks in through a door you didn't know you left open. (Credit for today's revelation goes to John Barrymore with the help of an old friend.)

20-year high school reunion...Here.We.Go! Heart Stomper had this quote as his status the week before and I thought it was quite telling considering a conversation we had just had. I decided to adopt it the night of our reunion because you just never know. It had been twenty years, two marriages and a hundred pounds since I'd seen him and most of my classmates. You never know where the next smile or heart pound might be hiding.

#331

Time is kind; it gently erases all the harsh memories and leaves in their place only the happy ones.

I could be a bitch. I could dish and dish about the reunion the night before, (I stayed relatively sober.) Who has changed for the worse, who hasn't changed at all but really should have, who got plastered and handsy in the limo and made an ass of himself. I could and it would be a *great* read! However, in the end, all that matters is that as the years gently slipped one into the other, we tended to only remember enough of the good 'ol days to annoy our children as we tell stories of the way things used to be. Well, I mean other peoples' kids because despite the fact I've recently had my uterus refurbished it's currently without a tenant. Probably because although I manage to do things like have two dates to the same event I get my freakin' period a few days before. I'm beginning to think it's a conspiracy.

Side Note: Do you have anybody in your life that makes you wonder what might have been? I did. The night of the reunion I found out what might have been and damn, I sure dodged a bullet.

Not that I wouldn't still give it another go…

Don't act so surprised, have you not been paying attention?

20 years Post-High School (Reunion) Revelation

November 28, 2010

#332

I tend to be a magnet for emotional drama and friends in crisis; often drunk, sometimes overnight.

There's a reason I sleep with the phone right next to my pillow and keep extra sheets, pillows and blankets in the living room closet.

November 29, 2010

#333

D'oh! Sometimes I *am* as dumb as I look...

Okay, true story. Even after sleeping on it for four months and fighting with the fitted sheet for just as long, I didn't realize that my bed was a Queen-size and not a full-size until Zach and I tried to put together my new bed frame so as to get the bed off of the floor. It's back on the floor for now.

#334

Love is stubborn and illogical; it is not susceptible to the Jedi Mind trick, compromise or bribery. Love stalks and sneaks up on you undetected, uninvited, uncontrolled and underestimated in its power.

Hey, Heart Stomper, are you paying attention? My boy, **Andrew,** encapsulated this perfectly, "'Love is the ultimate outlaw. It just won't adhere to any rules. The most any of us can do is to sign on as its accomplice. Instead of vowing to honor and obey, maybe we should swear to aid and abet. That would mean that security is out of the question. The words "make" and "stay" become inappropriate.' I'm not certain if any words have ever rung so true before."

20 years
Post-High School
Revelation

#335

Anything worth having in the first place should hurt like hell when it's gone.

If it doesn't hurt to lose it, was it ever really yours? Small wonder I ended the night sitting in my kitchen crying with one of my favorite drinking buddies.

#336

Today's revelation is a PSA for the fellas out there with a little help from my girl, Arazwo. She'll chase you for a while but there will come a day when she will stop running in circles around you. She's going to get over you and at that very moment, you're going to wish you had let her catch you.

It's a little humbling when someone half my age drops a nugget of wisdom on me like this. Would it be desperate and pathetic to have post cards printed with this one and send them to all the ones who got away? It would? Okay, how about just the top five? Three? Oh, come on, already!

#337

It's *always* a good idea at the time...

And I'm back in the saddle again.

#338

Lloyd Dobler set the gold standard.

What I'm about to admit here may set the women's movement back a hundred years but this project is about self-introspection, honesty and growth. If I ever looked out the window to see a former flame playing Peter Gabriel's *In Your Eyes* from an 80s boom box held over his head- rumpled trench coat optional- I'm sure I'd fall over backwards with my legs in the air. It is the mere hint of this possibility that drives me to wax on a regular basis even when I'm not seeing anybody special. I've admitted several times that I lean toward the dramatic and I've got a romantic side as big as my hair was back in high school. I admit it; I'm waiting for Lloyd and his Malibu to come sweep me off my feet. *sigh*

December 5, 2010

#339

I can dream, and in my dreams, I'm Christmasing with you. The Carpenters' song brought a tear to my eye the other day as I thought of the Christmas lights in Heaven and the people waiting for me on the other side. ❤

Christmas is a tough time of year for me. December 5, 1993, I lost my dad and he was Christmas' biggest fan. For seventeen years, I've been avoiding all things Christmas with every ounce of effort I could muster. The bitch of it is that no matter how hard I tried, Christmas would come and go whether I wanted it to or not. This year, I was determined to go with an "if you can't beat 'em, join 'em" attitude. There are people who have gone before me that I miss so much that I don't think even Lloyd Dobler himself could completely soothe the ache, but I'm not doing anyone any favors by dwelling on it and letting it own me. So, I can dream and love and miss them at the same time that I celebrate and honor their love for me by letting my joy eclipse my sorrow.

December 6, 2010

#340 If you want something to get done, ask the busiest person you know.

This was one of my dad's favorite sayings and I never realized how true it was until I became the busiest person I know.

December 7, 2010

#341 I still do my best work at the last minute.

I was slated to present two seminars this afternoon. I began prepping them this morning. I owned it.

December 8, 2010

#342 I can still pull an all-nighter and kick ass the next day!

So, fresh off my last-minute prep triumph, I'm chilling at home and think to myself, "I wonder how Tommy is feeling?" I shoot off a text and in return find that he's in the ER waiting for a CT scan. And off to the ER I go. Long story short, I help talk the twelve-year old they gave an MD to out of hacking him open in the hallway and sit on my ass listening to a sedated Tommy snore while waiting for security to come put his wallet and keys in the safe. I crawl into bed at 3:00 AM knowing full well I have time only for a quick nap before I have to get ready to go *back* to the same hospital and do a presentation for the board about my hospice. You'll never guess what happened next. ☺ Oh yeah, I owned that, too. Then I went home and took a long, long nap; I'm not in high school anymore, for crying out loud.

December 9, 2010

#343

Don Ready doesn't just sell cars, he has nine lives!

Don Ready could give Chuck Norris a run for his money.

December 10, 2010

#344

Look at the faces; Listen to the bells; It's hard to believe we need a place called hell. (Thanks, INXS)

Truth be told, I was stuck for a revelation and this song was stuck in my head. Also, I wanted a good excuse to change my profile picture to the one of me with the devil horns. Once again, if you think this is so easy *you* try it! I am a little disappointed with myself because I did manage to come up with something really cute a short while later that garnered a hilarious response. I'll share the good one with you, too, so you don't lose faith in me this close to the end.

Mia Semuta is feeling like going on a de-friending bender. Those on the possible cut list: 1. People who whine and complain about everything. 2. People playing the numbers game. 3. People who type in all caps. 4. People who have not brought a bottle to stock my new bar. 5. Cowboys' fans.

Trust me when I tell you that the commentary made me laugh so hard I peed a little.

December 11, 2010

#345

Fill your pockets with extra kindness and extra patience before you go out into the world; everybody is battling their own demons and could use a little back-up.

I worked at Bath & Body Works all through college. I was amazed year after year at the number of people who came to the mall in December and were genuinely shocked and annoyed that there were crowds of angry and frustrated people. Just in case you are unaware, allow me to enlighten you. Christmas is on the twenty-fifth *every* year. I used to get annoyed with them and let them affect my mood until I realized that what they needed was my help not my judgment. Now, before I venture out into public during the silly season, I load up on love to share and pass it out liberally. Here are my tips for holiday shopping survival:

- Wear comfortable shoes.
- Pee before you go.
- Take a bottle of water.
- Eat a decent meal at home.
- Take cash.
- Make frequent trips to the car so you don't have to schlep bags with you all over the mall.
- Hire a sitter and leave the kids at home.
- Make the cashier smile.

Oh, I still I hate shopping but even I survive it in December with a smile and nary a grey hair.

#346

Despite our best intentions we, as humans, do the most horrible and heinous things to the people we love the most. Our only sane choice is to forgive, forget and move on. Far too much energy is wasted living in our wounds and nurturing that anger.

Why do we do the awful things we do to one another? We really do seem to go out of our way to be horrible to one another, don't we?

#347

Believe in today; your life is now. (My baby sister taught me this one, thanks, Megan!!)

Megan, "Thanks for the reminder! I need to remember this every single day."

Is anybody else humming the John Cougar Mellencamp song in their head right now? No? Just me? Okay.

December 14, 2010

#348

There is an enormous divide between the number of people who think they are funny and the number of legitimately funny people. PS If you have to declare your own funniness...you're not funny.

If you're mentally preparing your defense of your funniness I'm thinking there's really no help for you.

December 15, 2010

#349

I have learned to pray differently. I still ask God for what I want but more importantly I ask for peace in my heart if it's not the right time for me to have it. It has made all the difference.

Seriously, I say some goofy shit but I mean it. I have so much more peace in my life than I used to.

December 16, 2010

#350

I've got a few talents so well-hidden even I didn't know about them!

I can crochet two dish rags in about three hours and make a hat that's almost kind of cute. Who knew?

#351

December 17, 2010

Sometimes, to be successful, you just have to suck the dick that's in front of you.

I told you, I'm in sales.

#352

December 18, 2010

I am rated R 85% of the time, occasionally even NC-17. This includes my facebook wall...

#353

December 19, 2010

You can either live in your wounds or learn from them.

Bet you can't guess which way I go.

#354

December 20, 2010

Lip gloss freezes when you leave it in the car overnight.

It's true! It feels kind of cool- pun intended- when you put it on your lips, too. ☺ My friend, **Ashlee**, tells me that it melts in the summer. She also laments the legions of chapstick that have sacrificed themselves for that bit of knowledge.

#355

I could give lessons on having fun.

One of the girls at my office, Adrienne, noted that she should take lessons on having fun from me. I thought about it and you know what? I could totally teach that master class.

December 22, 2010

#356

If I had it to do all over again I am certain I would make all the same mistakes but I would just get them out of the way much, much sooner.

Kelly, "Amen, sista, this is your best revelation yet."

Mia, "☺ some of my favorite mistakes I might even make twice..."

Hey, favorite mistakes, are you reading this? Call me.

#357

I have learned so much about gratitude and the importance of giving thanks. I am grateful today for a good job that fulfills me, a loving family that inspires me, fabulous friends that uplift me, precious pets that comfort me and the healing spirit that is allowing me to enjoy the silly season for the first time in 17 years.

Beth, "Hell...mutha fuckin'....YEAH!"

Tabitha, "Merry Christmas Mia. We love you."

Megan, "I'm just gonna 'like' this, because I don't think I can outdo Beth's comment. ☺"

Beth, "@Megan - So glad you know your place....MWAH!"

Remember a few revelations back when I declared my facebook wall rated-R? My friends know this, too, and they know it's a safe place to come and express themselves rated-R-style. As my friend, Beth, said to me the other day, "Sometimes I just need to be able to say 'fuck' on facebook and I know that on your wall I can do that." That you can, my friend; that you can.

#358

It's not about the presents under the tree; it's about the people around it.

Chastity, "aww!!!! im soooo stealing this!<will give you a shout out, however>"

Mia, "Chas, give the shout to my sister, Megan! ☺ She rocked this one for me. ❤"

Nora, "ABSOLUTELY, SISTA!!! MERRY CHRISTMAS!!! ☺"

Scott, "and about the wine not flowing like mud"

Mia, "The people around my tree are freakin' amazing! just sayin'"

Bunnie, "AMEN... XO to you and yours"

Mia, "Right back at ya, Aunt Bunnie! Scotty, the wine and the espresso martinis flowed in perfect harmony!"

My family celebrates on Christmas Eve. We always have since I was a little girl. Back then, we used to go to everybody's house, (we all lived very close to one another.) Now, we choose one house and have a nice big party and exchange gifts. This year, as part of my anti-Grinch plan, I volunteered to host Christmas Eve. Eight of my ten nieces and nephews, all of their parents, my grandparents, aunts and uncles and a few of my friends all ventured downtown in the city for Christmas Eve. I didn't want the kids up on the third floor. (The windows are easy to open and a kid splattered on the sidewalk puts a damper on the holiday spirit.) I told them that the third floor was the gateway to the North Pole and that Santa was taking a nap. If they woke him he would not come to their house later that night.

They totally bought it. How I miss the wonder and ignorance of youth. ☺ Zia loves you, my little darlings!

December 25, 2010

#359

I offer these gifts on this Christmas Day; to my opponents and enemies: tolerance and forgiveness. To my friends and family: my heart and my strength. To my patients and their families: service and patience. To every child: unconditional love. To everyone: compassion. To myself: respect.

Merry Christmas to one and all. And let us not forget that even Santa Claus takes time after a long, long night at work to remember the reason for the season. Happy Birthday, Jesus; thank you. ❤

December 26, 2010

#360

"Where two or three have gathered together in my name, I am there in their midst." Matthew 18:20

When our dad died, my siblings and I were blindsided and devastated. We'd lost touch over the years with others who had been important to Dad and who had loved him as much as we did. On the day after Christmas this year, we gathered together to have dinner with one of those people we'd lost touch with and in doing so I knew Dad was here with us again.

December 27, 2010

#361

Real women have curves; real smart women gather a support circle and tone them. Who wants in on a facebook Biggest Loser Club?

Twenty-five comments later a facebook group was created, rules agrees upon and Mia's Loser Friends was born. I'm thinking there's another book somewhere in this game.

December 28, 2010

#362

The most difficult piece of any task is not figuring out how to accomplish it, but the realization of what you will have to sacrifice for it.

One of the most basic concepts in economics is that of utility cost. We're not talking about the actual dollar amount of something, but whatever it is you'll have to give up for something else. Sadly, far too often it's time with the people that we love that we must spend to accomplish our goals.

#363

If women ruled the world there would be no wars just a bunch of angry, jealous countries not speaking to each other. Little shout out to my boy, Troy, for this little gem. Of course, I'm not speaking to him because I'm angry and jealous that he came up with this before I did...

If I'm being honest, I'll have to admit that I sat on this one for a good while because I didn't want it to be true. I tried to think of a way to refute it because I wanted women to be better than that. I wanted us to have risen above that, to have graduated high school. We haven't. But at least we can laugh at ourselves.

#364

December 30, 2010

Don't talk about it; be about it.

Put up or shut up, know what I'm sayin'?

#365

I still have so much more to learn.

Mia, "And, as if to really drive the point home, my nephew, Christopher, made me a great aunt this morning at 6:08 AM. Emma Marie, welcome!! ❤"

Pat, "Congrats to you and your nephew!"

Mia, "thanks, Pat!"

Tavia, "Ok, I have to ask....are you going to start your 21 years Post-High School Revelation tomorrow?"

Mia, "Tavia, I am not! Today's is the last. I am, however, happy to announce that the book of all of them with added commentary will be released on my birthday!"

Tavia, "haha...alright. and Yay for a book of them!"

Virginia, "I don't know, Mia; ONLY 1 year's worth? According to #365, you'll have so much more yet to share. ^-^ I know at my age, when I stop learning, I'll be dead! ❤"

Mia, "Ginny, it's been a interesting project and I might be willing to revisit it in a few years but I've come up with something insightful, interesting, poignant and/or funny every day for the past year. I'm glad I saw the project through, but I'm glad to be done! Writing the book has been a lot of fun, though. Expanding or giving the back story to the revelations and noticing patterns has been quite eye-opening!"

Virginia, "All right. You're allowed a 'breather' to refresh & restore your reservoir of wisdom; just don't wait too long. ^-^"

Karolyn, "Congrats on the new addition to the family!!!! And I didn't know you were making a book out of all these revelations, but I am definitely buying one when it's released!!!"

Mia, "Thanks, Karo! ☺"

Shane, "True True"

Kelly, "yep, we all do... that's why we're here. The blessing is to have those we love learn with us!"

Tom, "2011 will bless you all with "The World According to TA" Basically it will be a group of Plagiarized quotes slogan's with appropriate credit being given to the movie or book or singer. It will also consist of the occasional sprinkle of sentiment with a dash of Darwinism it should be interesting and result in at least some people defriending me or hiding my posts. ☺ Happy New Year!"

Mia, "Looking forward to it, Tommy!"

Michael, "@Tom in high school and college I lived for TA and now I get to look forward to it again"

I can't believe it's over.

In #s 147 and 264, I repeated the revelation, "Take pleasure in the details." Also, in #s 165 and 244, I repeated, "The waiting is the hardest part." And I'm so bummed that I did because as I was coming to the end I realized I had more revelations than days in the year. Damn 2010 not being a leap year!

As it turns out, since I doubled up I can offer one last revelation: **Don't be sorry, be aware.** Awareness in all aspects of your life and actions will help avoid a mountain of sorry. I'd also like to conclude with something really witty but I'm quite aware of how sorry I am that this project has come to an end. It was interesting and challenging, eye-opening and fun. Over the course of the year and this project, my facebook friends list more than doubled; I think it may have struck a nerve with a lot of people. I absolutely loved it. It's pretty late at night right now and I'm really sleepy, but I just don't want this to end.

Maybe I'll get drunk and call Heart Stomper.

I'll meet you back here in twenty years to tell you all about it.

~Mia

About the Author

Mia Semuta is the author of *Taking Chances* and the *Kaleidoscope* series. She earned her degrees from Kansas State, York College and Shippensburg University in English, History and English as a Second Language. Before becoming a published author, Mia was a high school teacher for ten years and explored careers in cooking and politics. Now enjoying a second career in Hospice care, she intends to continue to write about the world around her in the capital of Pennsylvania. With a life full of family, friends and felines she has no shortage of inspiration.

About the Artist

Pastiche is a graphic artist and grandmother with a self-described geek background in publishing and software development. She designs clip art, coloring pages and paper crafts to give away as free downloads and paper craft printables to families and teachers - free for personal or non-commercial use. A member of the Giant Squid 100 club, she has earned purple stars for several lenses. When not on Squidoo, she is blogging about Squidoo, drawing clip art and coloring pages and publishing Pastiche Family Portal. View her work by visiting www.leehansen.com

Also written by Mia Semuta

Taking Chances: A Love Story

Bianca DeAngelis, a woman in her mid-thirties, is ready to have a baby, but when she brings up the idea to her husband, he promptly divorces her, leaving her alone with their dog. She's just getting used to the idea of being single when she meets John Bennington, a former lawyer who shows up in Pennsylvania aiming to become a high school football coach. John has just gone through a divorce of his own, and without any sense of firm direction, he's set out to find a new one. When he botches up an appointment and gets caught in a winter storm, he is lucky enough to meet Bianca, who calls for a tow truck. They each feel an immediate attraction for each other, and there is plenty of chemistry! Join Bianca and John as they each try to overcome the obstacles that go along with former spouses, relatives, careers, and self-doubt. Both of them have one more shot at true love and happiness, but it all depends on Taking Chances.

Lost & Found

Engaged to be married and by all appearances the perfect couple, Emily Eldridge and Jason Patterson unbury a secret that threatens to destroy their future and must face the realities of life in modern America to decide if a lifetime of apparent perfection is really enough to live for.

Grief can not be contained. It can be denied and delayed, but eventually it will burst out of its confinement to take its toll. Debts paid in cash, no matter how deep, are effortless compared to the balance due Death.

The Book of Revelations

A year's worth of facebook wisdom

For one calendar year, Mia Semuta made daily observations about things that she has learned- either by choice or circumstance- in the twenty years since high school. Each of these revelations was posted as a facebook status and she developed a loyal following to her frequently witty, sometimes sobering, often controversial but always honest inspections of herself and the world around her.

On New Year's Eve the revelations were collected; some were given the back story or expanded upon, others carried the comments from her readers. Finally, some simply stood on their own in their humor, insight and raw sincerity. It's been twenty years since high school, what have you learned?